Praise for
TRANSFORMATION

This book will become one of the greatest tools throughout Christendom to teach new Christians. It is loaded with the methodological application of practicality for the spirituality. Trina has been able to capture the simplicity of achieving an effectively meaningful and contagious walk with the Most High God. This book also serves as one of the most complete teaching manuals I have observed on the market that addresses the process of salvation and how to maintain it after the altar experience. For the seasoned Christian, this book will help keep the salvation experience freshly embedded in the soul and will perpetuate a closer walk with Jesus Christ, the Son of the living God. Last, this book will serve as a blueprint to build a mighty army of witnesses so that neighborhoods, cities, and nations will be transformed.

SONYA T. ELLERBE
Senior Pastor
United Christian Fellowship Church International
Salisbury, North Carolina

Transformation will be a wonderful contribution to the field of Christian education and the study of theology. The exegesis of the sacred texts that pertain to salvation is accurate and demonstrates theological scholarship. I expect this work to add to and possibly replace many of the existing catechism manuals for new converts and church members. The details given that address the various aspects of salvation reflect the obvious hours of research and prayer invested in this project. As the founder and president of Charlotte Life Christian University, I would not hesitate to recommend this material for the training and educating of church leaders, especially senior pastors and overseers.

DR. STEVEN T. MILLER
Charlotte Life Christian University
Charlotte, North Carolina

TRANSFORMATION

Transformation Leader Edition by Trina Nichelle Moore

Published by
Degel Publishing
PO Box 621606
Charlotte, NC 28262
www.trinanichellemoore.com

All rights reserved solely by the author. This book is protected by the copyright laws of the United States of America. The author guarantees all contents are original and do not infringe upon the legal rights of any other person or work.

No part of this book may be reproduced or transmitted in any form or by any means, electronic or mechanical—including photocopying, recording, or by any information storage and retrieval system—without permission in writing from the publisher. Please direct your inquiries to the following: Degel Publishing, Attn: Permissions Editor, PO Box 621606, Charlotte, NC 28262.

All Scripture is taken from the New King James Version (NKJV) unless otherwise notated.

Scripture quotations marked (NKJV) are taken from the New King James Version®. Copyright © 1982 by Thomas Nelson, Inc. Used by permission. All rights reserved.

Scripture quotations marked (AMP) are taken from the Amplified® Bible,
Copyright © 1954, 1958, 1962, 1964, 1965, 1987 by The Lockman Foundation
Used by permission." (www.Lockman.org)

Scriptures marked KJV are taken from the King James Version Bible.

Scriptures quotations marked (NLT) are taken from the Holy Bible, New Living Translation copyright © 1996, 2004, 2007 by Tyndale House Foundation. Used by permission of Tyndale House Publishers Inc., Carol Stream, Illinois 60188. All rights reserved. New Living, NLT, and the New Living Translation logo are registered trademarks of Tyndale House Publishers.

© 2015 by Trina Nichelle Moore

International Standard Book Number: 978-0-9963232-2-2
Library of Congress Control Number: 2015906645

Dedication

This book is dedicated to every person who desires to understand what it truly means to be a victorious Christian. It is for those who desire to experience the Father's unconditional love and live a life fully yielded to Him. It is dedicated to individuals who yearn to be delivered from the bondages of sin and live a liberated and abundant life in Christ. It is for those who are hungry to be *TRANSFORMED!*

ACKNOWLEDGMENTS

I would like to acknowledge God for gifting me with His grace to write this curriculum. Becoming an author was not a goal I believed was possible. With God ALL things are possible!

I would first like to honor and acknowledge my parents, Mr. Robert Moore and Ms. Mary Hall. Your standards of raising me in a Christian home have made this possible. Thank you for making Sunday school a part of my childhood church experience. This is where my biblical knowledge was cultivated and developed for eighteen years. The spiritual foundation you laid has been a springboard for God to fulfill His perfect will in my life.

I would like to acknowledge Ms. Gloria Feaster for completing the initial editing and proofreading. I would also like to acknowledge Ms. Katharine Vail for completing the final edits. Thank you both for serving the body of Christ with your assistance. May the blessings of the Lord overtake you!

Last, but certainly not least, I acknowledge my spiritual mentor in ministry, Pastor Sonya T. Ellerbe. Thank you for truly fulfilling the call of a pastor. The rich oil of God's Word is poured into the flock of United Christian Fellowship Church International every week without reservation or fail. By receiving the Word of God that is preached, I gained the theological knowledge and understanding that adequately equipped me to complete this curriculum. You acknowledged the call of God on my life in the equipping ministry of the teacher and provided opportunities to mature my abilities to effectively minister God's Word.

PART ONE

Individual Edition

TRANSFORMATION

Maximize Salvation

TRINA NICHELLE MOORE

CONTENTS

Introduction 1
How to Use Transformation 3

Chapter 1 *What Is Salvation and Why Is It Necessary?*
What Is Salvation? 7
Why Is Salvation Necessary? 9
Initial Reception of Salvation 20
Salvation Regenerates 21
Salvation Is for the *Whole* Person: Spirit, Soul, and Body 23
The Eternal Result 25
How to Receive Salvation 26

Chapter 2 *Get Connected, Stay Connected*
Maintaining Your *God* Connection 32
Connection 1 – Find the Right Church and Become Planted 32
Connection 2 – Remain Distraction Free 36
Connection 3 – Study of God's Word 38
Connection 4 – Prayer: Dialogue with God 40
Connection 5 – Fellowship with Other Christians 42
Suggested Prayer and Study Practices 43
Necessary Study Tools for All Christians 44

Chapter 3 *Maintaining Salvation*
Why Must I Maintain A Free Gift? 48
Christians and Sinners 53
Repentance 58
What Is Grace? 63
Fasting 65
What If I Still Have Issues After I Become a Christian? 70
Seven Steps to Maintain Salvation 73

Chapter 4 *The Trinity: Father, Son, and Holy Spirit*
    The Function of the Father 80
    The Function of the Son.. 80
    The Function of the Holy Spirit.. 80

Chapter 5 *The Holy Spirit*
    Who Is the Holy Spirit?... 85
    The Function of the Holy Spirit.. 86
    Baptism of the Holy Spirit 86
    What Are Tongues? 86
    When Can Tongues (the Heavenly Language) Be Spoken? 87
    Benefits of Speaking in Tongues 88
    How to Receive the Baptism of the Holy Spirit 91

Chapter 6 *The Holy Spirit: The Gifts of the Spirit*
    Revelatory Gifts: Word of Knowledge, Word of Wisdom,
        Discerning of Spirits, Prophecy 96
    Miraculous Gifts: Gift of Faith, Gift of Healing, Working of Miracles 96
    Utterance Gifts: Different Kinds of Tongues, Interpretation of Tongues.......... 97

Chapter 7 *Becoming A New Person in Christ*
    The Human Trichotomy: Spirit, Soul, Body......................................102
    The Three Parts of the Soul: Will, Mind, and Emotions...................103
    The Physical Body 104

Notes 109

INTRODUCTION

What a privilege to know Jesus Christ as Savior! It is my passion to bring clarity to the Word of God in a simplistic form that takes one through the process of understanding to life application. Jesus came to give us life more abundantly! Christians cannot have abundant life if biblical principles are not put into action.

My prayer for everyone who ventures into this study is that you may draw closer to the Father knowing you are His beloved son or daughter. May His love draw you into a rich, intimate, and loving relationship that produces a thirst to become a new creature in Christ. May your passion be renewed to share His love with those who need to know Him.

Prepare to be equipped, empowered, and *TRANSFORMED* through this time of impartation and study!

HOW TO USE
TRANSFORMATION

The *Transformation* curriculum is written in workbook style. It is designed to be an interactive study of the foundational principles of Christianity that can be used for private individual study, small group study, Sunday school, or Bible study classes. Every chapter has assessment questions after each section. If you cannot correctly answer the questions return to the section's reading passage and review. All questions are in reading order.

The *Transformation Leader Edition* should be purchased if the curriculum is going to be used in a small group setting, Sunday school, or Bible study. The *Transformation Leader Edition* includes *Transformation* at the beginning of the book for personal use and teaching outlines for instructional use. It is *highly* recommended that each teacher or leader complete the individual study prior to presenting to a group. The teaching outline includes:

- ✓ **Each chapter outlined for teaching purposes**
- ✓ **The answers for each section highlighted within the outline**
- ✓ **The answers listed in the question-and-answer section**
- ✓ **Group leader suggestions for group activities and discussions**

If your church has ministerial staff, leaders, teaching departments, or individuals who need training, the author is available to conduct training sessions. Complete the contact form at www.trinanichellemoore.com.

CHAPTER 1

What Is Salvation and Why Is It Necessary?

WHAT IS SALVATION?

When asked this question, most Christians state that salvation is accepting Jesus as Lord with a reward of eternal life in heaven. While the aforementioned is true, this chapter will examine the holistic nature of salvation for those who believe and receive Jesus Christ as Lord. While salvation saves one from sin and eternal punishment in hell, it is also intended to be in perpetual (continuous) existence in the earthly life of a Christian. This includes spiritual, emotional, and physical issues as well as any difficult or challenging circumstances one may be facing.

Salvation is deliverance and preservation from sin and its effects, illusion (incorrect perceptions), and destruction (physical/emotional harm, wrong decisions, or anything that is destructive). Salvation also regenerates. To *regenerate* is to remake; restoring to a better state of existence. Therefore, it can be concluded that salvation ***delivers and preserves from sin and its effects, illusion, and destruction, restoring to a better state of existence.*** Salvation is holistic. The spirit, soul (will, mind, emotions), and body can experience salvation. It can make those who have received Jesus Christ *whole*. To be ***whole*** is ***to be made complete and entire lacking nothing.***

Think of an antique piece of furniture that is worn down and not in condition to be used nor seen. This piece of furniture will need to be restored before it is displayed or ready for use. If we allow God (the restorer) into our lives, salvation will remake and restore us to pristine condition (John 10:10).[1]

It is very important to understand that salvation cannot be earned through effort or works. Salvation is given to those who confess and believe by faith (Romans 10:9-10). But it does not excuse a Christian from displaying the fruit of their salvation. The fruit, or evidence, of salvation is obedience to the Word of God and the display of godly character (Galatians 5:22-26). The above stated is a direct result of a Christian maintaining their salvation, which is explained in detail in chapter 3.

Definition of Salvation

Salvation is *deliverance* and *preservation* from sin, illusion, and destruction, restoring to a better state of existence.

Questions and Answers

1. What is salvation?

    Salvation is _____ and _____ from _____, _____ and _____, restoring to a _____ state of existence.

2. What does salvation save you from?

    a. _____
    b. _____
    c. _____

✓ Self-Check

3. What areas in your life need to experience salvation (regeneration)?

    _____
    _____
    _____
    _____
    _____
    _____
    _____

WHY IS SALVATION NECESSARY?

Adam, Eve, and Sin

God created the first humans, Adam and Eve, to dwell in His presence. He created a beautiful garden, the Garden of Eden, for Adam and Eve to live (Genesis 2:8-25). God gave them free rein of the garden, but they were not to eat from the tree of knowledge of good and evil (Genesis 2:16-17). The serpent tempted Adam and Eve to disobey God (Genesis 3). This one act of disobedience to God created a legal opening for the results of sin to reign in the earth (Genesis 3:14-19).

Sin is any action that is contrary to the Word of God. Obedience and disobedience can manifest two different outcomes. Godly obedience manifests the blessings (goodness) of God (Deuteronomy 28:1-14). One of the most important benefits of God's blessings is the privilege and access to have a supernatural connection with God ALL the time. You can talk to God, and God will talk back to you. This connection will also provide you with everything needed during each and every season and circumstance that may occur in your life. Other examples of blessings include (but are not limited to) prosperity, peace, healing, provision, miracles, contentment, and favor.

On the other hand, disobedience manifests curses (opposite of blessings). Examples of curses include (but are not limited to) lack, poverty, sickness, disease, discontentment, strife, contention, and bondage (Deuteronomy 28:15-24). When Adam and Eve disobeyed God, their actions provided a legal opening for curses to manifest. Genesis 3:14-24 depicts how the curse will manifest. Those manifestations in Genesis 3 included pain in childbearing, hardened soil, death, and eviction from the Garden of Eden. This curse broke the connection (relationship) between Adam and Eve and God, separating them from His presence.

Sin and iniquity now have legal access in the earth. This is not God's fault, but the result of Adam and Eve's disobedience. Humans would have had to endure the consequences of Adam and Eve's sin, which is death on earth and eternity with Satan. Even now, no one is exempt from death, but we have an option with our eternal resting place. This option is eternal life made possible through Jesus Christ. You are probably asking the question: How did Jesus provide options to our eternal resting place? Let's go back to Genesis to find the answer.

Humans Have Earthly Dominion

> *Let Us make man in Our image, according to Our likeness; let them have dominion over the fish of the sea, over the birds of the air, and over the cattle, over all the earth and over every creeping thing that creeps on the earth. So God created man in His own image; in the image of God He created him; male and female He created them.*
> GENESIS 1:26-27

For God to have authority in the earth He must have a human in agreement with His perfect will. God established this in Genesis 1:26-27 when He gave mankind dominion over all the earth. God is the creator of all things. Therefore, He should be able to do anything He desires with complete control, right? In theory, the answer is yes. In reality, the answer is no. I want to review examples in the Scriptures to prove that God needs a human in agreement to fulfill His will on earth.

If My People

> *If My people, who are called by My name, will humble themselves, and pray and seek My face, and turn from their wicked ways, then I will hear from heaven, and will forgive their sin and heal their land. Now My eyes will be open and My ears attentive to prayer made in this place.*
> 2 CHRONICLES 7:14-15

In this passage of Scripture, God is responding to Solomon's prayer of dedication (2 Chronicles 6:12-42) for the temple Israel built to worship Him. In 2 Chronicles 7:12, God appeared to Solomon to confirm that He indeed heard his prayer. Solomon's prayer would be answered if Israel did the following: 1) humble themselves, 2) pray, 3) seek His face, and 4) turn from their wicked ways. If Israel did the aforementioned, God would 1) hear from heaven, 2) forgive their sin, and 3) heal their land (v.14). Obedience releases God to move on our behalf. In 2 Chronicles 7:19-22, God gives a warning to Israel of what would occur if they did not adhere to the instructions in verse 14.

> *"But if you turn away and forsake My statutes and My commandments which I have set before you, and go and serve other gods, and worship them, then I will uproot them from My land which I have given them; and this house which I have sanctified for My name I will cast out of My sight, and will make it a proverb and a byword among all peoples.*
>
> *And as for this house, which is exalted, everyone who passes by it will be astonished and say, 'Why has the Lord done thus to this land and this house?' Then they will answer, 'Because they forsook the Lord God of their fathers, who brought them out of the land of Egypt, and embraced other gods, and worshiped them and served them; therefore He has brought all this calamity on them.'"*

No One to Stand in the Gap

> *"The people of the land have used oppressions, committed robbery, and mistreated the poor and needy; and they wrongfully oppress the stranger. So I sought for a man among them who would make a wall, and stand in the gap before Me on behalf of the land, that I should not destroy it; but I found no one... and I have recompensed their deeds on their own heads," says the Lord God.*   Ezekiel 22:29-31

In this passage of Scripture, God was searching for a qualified leader to move the hearts of the people away from sin. The phrase **make a wall** is metaphoric imagery meaning that God needed a person with enough spiritual influence to turn Israel (God's chosen people) back to God. This leader would need to be one who exemplified a life of godly obedience and could teach the people to do the same. He could not find a suitable leader. As a result (v.31), the people reaped the consequences of sin.

Power of Agreement

> *Again, I say to you that if two of you agree on earth concerning anything that they ask, it will be done for them by My Father in heaven. For where two or three are gathered together in my name, I am there in the midst of them.*   MATTHEW 18:19-20

This Scripture states that if two individuals agree concerning what they need from the Lord it will be done. Jesus also continues to state that He will be in the midst of those purposely gathered together (in agreement) in His name. It must also be noted that those coming together in agreement must petition God according to His will. 1 John 5:14-15 states, *"Now this is the confidence that we have in Him, that if we ask anything according to His will, He hears us. And if we know that He hears us, whatever we ask, we know that we have the petitions that we have asked of Him."*

It is also important to note that the will of God must be spiritually discerned according to individual circumstances and the timing of God. James 4:3 says, *"You ask and do not receive, because you ask **amiss**, that you may spend it on your pleasures."* This Scripture brings out the important fact that prayers should *not* be prayed based upon personal agenda, but according to the perfect will of God for each situation.

Let's use a practical example. You are praying for a spouse. There is absolutely nothing wrong with having a desire to marry. God created the institution of marriage. Genesis 2:18 says, *"It is not good that man should be alone; I will make him a helper comparable to him."* You notice an individual of the opposite sex that catches your eye and you begin to pray that that person becomes your spouse. *Stop!* You should first ask God if that person is the spouse He has ordained for you. If God reveals that person is not the spouse He has ordained you are praying *amiss* because that is what you want. You are praying according to the *scriptural* will but not the **perfect** will of God. Though it is correct based upon Scripture, it may not be aligned to the perfect will of God ordained for you.

It must be understood that God strategically orders our steps and places people in our paths to fulfill the perfect will of God for our lives. Ultimately, this will further the Kingdom of God. The *perfect will of God* must be known and acted upon.

Preach the Gospel

And He said to them, "Go into all the world and preach the gospel to every creature."

MARK 16:15

How then shall they call on Him in whom they have not believed? And how shall they believe in Him of whom they have not heard? And how shall they hear without a preacher?

ROMANS 10:14

God is not coming down from heaven to preach the gospel. He commissioned the disciples in Mark 16:15 to do so. Christians, in present times, are disciples (followers of Christ) and are also commissioned to share the gospel.

Not Willing that Any Should Perish

> *The Lord is not slack concerning His promise, as some count slackness, but is longsuffering toward us, not willing that any should perish but that all should come to repentance.*
>
> 2 PETER 3:9

This Scripture states that God does not want anyone to perish in his or her sins. He is long-suffering and kind toward us, but He does not excuse sin. Are not people perishing in their sins because they choose not to repent (turn away) from sinful behavior? Yes. If an individual chooses not to follow the way of the Lord they will reap the consequences of their decision.

Salvation

> *That if **you** confess with **your** mouth the Lord Jesus and believe in **your** heart that God has raised Him from the dead, **you** will be saved. For with the heart one believes unto righteousness, and with the mouth confession is made unto salvation.*
>
> ROMANS 10:9-10

Salvation is received based upon the individual making the decision to accept. The Scripture states, "That if **you** confess with **your** mouth..." God is not going to force Himself on anyone. Salvation is freely given so that it can be willfully and freely received.

Practical Example

I want to use a practical example to further explain that God needs a human in agreement to fulfill His will on earth. In our modern society the most common mode of transportation is a car. In order to get from point A to point B, the driver must get in the car, turn it on, and drive to the desired destination. A car cannot travel unless there is someone willing to drive. The will of God is the car. God created humans to do (drive) His will. Christians (driver) are to fulfill God's will; however, He has specific directions (Scriptures) regarding how to get to and from various destinations. Though Christians are the drivers, they are to follow God's directions. God is in control through Christians (humans) in agreement with His will. To sum it up, the will of God is the car, humans are the drivers, God is the GPS!

Questions and Answers

1. What caused the need for salvation?

   _____
   _____

2. Genesis 1:26-27 says, "Let Us make man in Our image, according to our likeness; let them have _____ over the fish of the sea, over the birds of the air, and over the cattle, _____ and over every creeping thing that creeps on the earth. So God created man in His own image; in the image of God He created him; _____ and _____ He created them.

3. For God to have _____ in the earth He must have a _____ in _____ with His perfect will.

4. In 2 Chronicles 7:14-15 what four actions did Israel need to display for their prayers to be answered?
   a. _____
   b. _____
   c. _____
   d. _____

5. List at least three Scriptural references from this section that confirm that God needs a human in agreement to fulfill His perfect will.

   _____
   _____
   _____

✓ Self-Check

6. What has God told you to do (that you have not done) to get in alignment with His word?

   _____
   _____
   _____
   _____
   _____
   _____
   _____
   _____
   _____
   _____
   _____
   _____
   _____
   _____
   _____
   _____

Jesus, the Unblemished Human

Back to the question of origin: How did Jesus provide options to our eternal resting place? Since humans severed the relationship with God through acts of sin, it was necessary for God to have a human to restore it. God sent His Son, Jesus, to earth as a human through the virgin birth for the ultimate purpose of taking away the sins of the world. Jesus had to be in agreement with the will of God to die for our sins.

> *Father, if it is Your will, take this cup away from Me; nevertheless not My will, but Yours, be done. Then an angel appeared to Him from heaven, strengthening Him.*
>
> LUKE 22:42-43

Luke captures the brief moment in which Jesus did not want to go to the cross. He had a moment of humanity. However, His humanity did not cause Him to disobey. He overcame the flesh and began to operate in the spirit (Romans 8:5). Jesus understood that He was God's solution to the sin problem. Once He refocused Himself on the assignment an angel appeared strengthening Him (Luke 22:43). God will always provide what is needed to do His will.

God needed an unblemished human to take away the sins of the world. That unblemished human was Jesus Christ. Jesus was born as a human through Mary who was a virgin. It was a supernatural conception. In other words, no human egg or sperm had anything to do with conceiving Jesus. The crucifixion of Christ paid the final penalty of sin for the entire human race (Isaiah 53). Again, the penalty of sin is death on earth and eternity with Satan. Jesus Christ took the penalty in our place. This is how Jesus provided an option to our eternal resting place. Choosing Jesus is choosing eternal life!

As noted, God needs a human in agreement with His perfect will. Can you imagine having to sacrifice a loved one for a greater cause? You would most likely try to find an alternative solution. God knew He gave humans dominion over the earth. Therefore, a human in agreement with His plan of redemption was necessary to restore the relationship between God and mankind through salvation. He demonstrated such integrity that He would not go against His own word even if it meant that His Son, Jesus, would have to die for our sins (Psalm 138:2). In other words, God did not change the rules in the best interest of His Son. He honored His word above His own personal interest. He sent His Son to die so those who believe can receive the ultimate benefits of salvation. Isaiah 53:10 says, *"Yet it pleased the Lord to bruise Him."* Now that is *selfless* love!

Jesus' death on the cross symbolizes the end of the reign of sin and its destruction in the life of a Christian. Before Jesus Christ (Old Testament), the priests of God were required to sacrifice an unblemished animal to atone for human sin. Jesus (the High Priest) was the final unblemished sacrifice for the atonement of sin for all of mankind. His crucifixion paid the final penalty for our sins (Hebrews 9:1-15). The natural act following death is burial. Jesus' burial is symbolic of sin being buried or done away with.

If we receive salvation we have another chance to overcome from the grips of sin. Finally, Jesus' miraculous resurrection from the grave proves that He is the Savior of the world and He came to give new life abundantly (John 10:10). The resurrection is symbolic of becoming new in Christ and the new covenant of salvation God has afforded to those who believe (Romans 10:9-10; 2 Corinthians 5:17). This redemption has restored the relationship between God and mankind as it was with Adam and Eve before sin. Now a relationship is attainable through receiving the gift of salvation through Jesus Christ.

Jesus Christ became us when He took our sins on the cross. Through His redemption, those who receive Him will become new in Him. Salvation makes us one with Christ. Therefore, we are joint heirs with Him with all of heaven's resources open to us. Jesus Christ prayed this in Matthew 6:10, "Your kingdom come. Your will be done on earth as it is in heaven."

> *The Spirit Himself bears witness with our spirit that we are children of God, and if children, then heirs—heirs of God and joint heirs with Christ, if indeed we suffer with Him, that we may also be glorified together.* ROMANS 8:16-17

> *For there is one God and one Mediator between God and men, the man Christ Jesus, who gave Himself a ransom for all.* 1 TIMOTHY 2:5-6

> *The thief does not come except to steal, and to kill, and to destroy. I have come that they may have life, and that they may have it more abundantly.* JOHN 10:10

> *Therefore, if anyone is in Christ, he is a new creation; old things have passed away; behold, all things have become new.* 2 CORINTHIANS 5:17

It is important to understand that Jesus was truly human in spirit, soul, and body. He did not have any special privileges or powers when He came to earth because He was the Son of God. He was stripped of his godly deity. Hebrews 4:15 says, *"[He] was in all points tempted as we are, yet without sin."* While on earth Jesus had the potential to sin, was tempted by sin, but did not sin. Not only was it Jesus' purpose to come to earth and take away the sins of the world, but He was the ultimate example of how to live a victorious life without sin. He was able to do so because He loved His Father (God) above anything else.

Love is a choice with the appropriate actions displayed. John 14:15 says, *"If you love Me, keep My commandments."* God is love (1 John 4:8). In the beginning was the Word, and the Word was God (John 1:1). God is love, and God is the Word. Therefore, to love God means to keep His commandments, for His commandments are His written Word. In simple terms, **DO** the Word. If the Word says repent, then you do it. If it says love your neighbor, then do it. If it says pray and study the Scriptures, then be obedient and do it. I believe you get the point!

Second, Jesus knew sinful behavior would not please His Father, nor was it in the commandments (Word of God). He knew it was absolutely necessary to maintain a consistent connection with His Father so He would be strong enough to resist sin. This connection is what gave Him the power He needed to be obedient and to stay focused on fulfilling His assignment (death, burial, and resurrection).

WHAT IS SALVATION AND WHY IS IT NECESSARY?

Questions and Answers

1. Why was it necessary for Jesus to come to earth as a human?

   _____
   _____
   _____

2. What do the death (crucifixion), burial, and resurrection symbolize?

   a) Death (crucifixion): _____
   _____

   b) Burial: _____
   _____

   c) Resurrection: _____
   _____

3. Did Jesus have any special privileges as the Son of God while He was on earth?

   _____
   _____
   _____

4. How was Jesus able to live a victorious life without sin?

   _____
   _____
   _____

5. John 14:15 states, _____
   _____.

INITIAL RECEPTION OF SALVATION

That if you confess with your mouth the Lord Jesus and believe in your heart that God has raised Him from the dead, you will be saved. For with the heart one believes unto righteousness, and with the mouth confession is made unto salvation.

ROMANS 10:9-10

This passage of Scripture explains how to receive salvation. One must **confess** and **believe** in Jesus Christ and **make Him Lord** in his or her life. When one confesses Jesus as Lord, He becomes the final authority in a Christian's life. This means there is complete obedience to the Word of God. For a more in-depth review, read the passage of Scripture below taken from the Amplified Bible:

*Because if you acknowledge and confess with your lips that Jesus is Lord and in your heart (innermost being) believe (adhere to, trust in and rely on truth) that God raised him from the dead, you will be **delivered and preserved**. For with the heart (innermost being) a person believes (adheres to, trusts in and relies on truth) and so is justified (declared righteous, acceptable to God), and with the mouth he confesses (declares openly and speaks out freely his faith) and confirms [his] **deliverance and preservation**.*

ROMANS 10:9-10, AMP, EMPHASIS ADDED

Questions and Answers

1. How does a person receive salvation?

    a. _____

    b. _____

    c. _____

SALVATION REGENERATES

I want to review another Scripture passage that speaks of salvation. As stated in the beginning of this chapter, another word or synonym for salvation is *regenerate*. To *regenerate* is to **remake: restoring to a better state of existence**. In John 3, Jesus explains salvation to a Pharisee, Nicodemus, using the terminology **born again**. In John 3:16, Jesus speaks of believing in Him and the work of the cross before it even happened. *"For God so loved the world that He gave His only begotten Son, that whoever believes in Him should not perish but have everlasting life."* Jesus knew His purpose! The definition of **born again** is explained below in greater detail.

> *Jesus answered, "Most assuredly, I say to you, unless one is born of water and the Spirit, he cannot enter the kingdom of God. That which is born of the flesh is flesh, and that which is born of the Spirit is spirit. Do not marvel that I said to you, **'You must be born again.'** The wind blows where it wishes, and you hear the sound of it, but cannot tell where it comes from and where it goes. So is everyone who is born of the Spirit."*
>
> JOHN 3:5-8

Born: To bring forth or brought forth
Again (*Anothen* in Greek): From above, from a higher place; anew, over again[2]
Regenerate: To remake; restoring to a better state of existence
Born again: Brought forth anew to a better state of existence

Now read John 3:5-8 with the definition of **born again** as stated above:

> *Most assuredly, I say to you, unless one is **brought forth anew** of water and the Spirit, he cannot enter the kingdom of God. That which is **brought forth** of the flesh is flesh, and that which is **brought forth** of the Spirit is spirit. Do not marvel that I said to you, 'You must be **brought forth anew**.' The wind blows where it wishes, and you hear the sound of it, but cannot tell where it comes from and where it goes. So is everyone who is **brought forth** of the Spirit.*

Another Scripture verse that supports the newness that accompanies salvation is 2 Corinthians 5:17, *"Therefore, if any man be in Christ he is a new creation; old things have passed away; behold, all things have become new."*

Questions and Answers

1. What does it mean to be born again?

_____
_____
_____
_____

SALVATION IS FOR THE *WHOLE* PERSON: SPIRIT, SOUL, AND BODY

A Christian receives salvation when he or she confesses and believes in Jesus Christ (Romans 10:9-10). A Christian can also experience salvation beyond the point of praying the prayer of salvation. Salvation is everlasting (perpetual, enduring) in nature. It first occurs spiritually (by receiving Jesus as Lord; salvation) and should bear fruit in the natural (behavior). The saving power of Jesus can and should be a perpetual experience in the life of a Christian. This can only happen when a Christian is **consistently connected** and **obedient** to the Word of God. Hebrews 4:12 proves that God (John 1:1) desires that His saving grace make us clean and whole in every area.

> *For the Word that God speaks is alive and full of power [making it active, operative, energizing and effective]; it is sharper than any two-edged sword, penetrating to the dividing line of the breath of life (soul) and [the immortal] spirit, and of joints and marrow [of the deepest parts of our nature], exposing and sifting and analyzing and judging the very thoughts and purposes of the heart.* HEBREWS 4:12, AMP

The definition of salvation stated at the beginning of this chapter, and in Hebrews 4:12, establishes that salvation is for all parts that make up the human being: spirit, soul (will, mind, emotions), and body. Therefore, the effects of salvation make the person who receives **whole**. To be whole is **to be made entire and complete, lacking nothing**. The word **made** indicates there is a process to becoming whole. When something is made, a process must be followed before the finished product can be presented. The results are not always instant. Be willing to take the time to experience salvation in those areas of difficulty. Galatians 6:9 states, *"And let us not grow weary while doing good, for in due season we shall reap if we do not lose heart."*

Due season does not have a time limit because it can be different for each individual. James 1:4 says, *"But let patience have its perfect work, that you may be perfect and complete, lacking nothing."* The Lord knows what it is going to take for each of His children to be complete and lacking nothing. Do not be afraid to exercise patience. Salvation is not magic. Be willing to yield to the salvation process and see the results manifested in your life.

Questions and Answers

1. How can a Christian experience the perpetual (enduring) benefits of salvation?

   _____
   _____
   _____

2. What makes up the whole person?

   _____
   _____
   _____

3. What does it mean to be made whole?

   _____
   _____
   _____

4. The word _____ indicates there is a _____ to becoming whole.

5. Galatians 6:9 says, _____
   _____

6. _____ _____ does not have a time limit because it can be different for each individual.

7. James 1:4 says, _____
   _____

THE ETERNAL RESULT

There is an eternal result of salvation. It is the inheritance of eternal life with God once this earthly life is over. Those who are unsaved will spend eternity in hell with Satan.

Heaven
Heaven is the place where God, Jesus, and the Holy Spirit live. All Christians who believe in Jesus Christ and fulfill His will are rewarded with eternal life in heaven.
See Revelation 22:14; Matthew 25:46; John 3:3-7, 4:14, 5:24, 8:51, 11:25-26.

Hell
Those who do not believe, do not accept Jesus as Lord nor obey His commands will be sent to hell to suffer for eternity.
See Matthew 25:41-43; 2 Peter 2:3-9; Revelation 19:20; Mark 16:16; Romans 13:2;
1 Corinthians 6:8-10; Galatians 5:19-21; 1 Timothy 5:12.

HOW TO RECEIVE SALVATION

If you are reading this book and have not accepted the Lord Jesus Christ as your personal Savior, please read the "Steps to Receive Salvation" section below and pray the prayer of salvation. If you were once saved and have turned away from God, you also can pray the prayer of salvation and recommit your life to the Lord. Remember that it is not your actions that produce salvation. It is believing, confessing, and receiving Jesus as Lord (sole authority) in your life.

Steps to Receive Salvation

1. **Admit** that you have sinned, confess (to God) your sins and repent (turn away from sin).*

2. **Believe** in your heart (innermost being, spirit, the real you) that Jesus Christ died for your sins and God raised Him from the dead.

3. **Confess** (speak aloud) that Jesus Christ is Lord in your life.

4. Immediately begin attending a Bible-based, Holy Spirit-filled church.

Prayer of Salvation

Lord Jesus Christ, I am sorry for the things I have done wrong in my life. I ask your forgiveness and now turn (repent) from everything I know is wrong according to the Word of God. I believe You died on the cross to set me free from my sins and were resurrected so that I can have a new life in You. Please come into my life and fill me with Your Holy Spirit. Amen.

Praise God! If you have prayed the prayer of salvation make it a priority to *immediately* get connected with other strong Christians and begin attending a Spirit-filled church that teaches the Word of God in truth. Read more about getting connected in the next chapter. Chapter 3 "Maintaining Salvation" will take you through the steps of applying salvation into every area of your life.

*Refer to the section on Repentance in chapter 3 for an in depth explanation.

CHAPTER 2

Get Connected, Stay Connected

GET CONNECTED, STAY CONNECTED

Once a commitment is made to Christianity, it is vitally important to stay connected to God. Many individuals commit their lives to the Lord without immediately connecting with a church and other strong Christians. As a result, they find themselves spiritually weak and uncommitted to the Lord. Hebrews 10:24-25 says, *"And let us consider one another in order to stir up love and good works, not forsaking the assembling of ourselves together, as is the manner of some, but exhorting one another, and so much the more as you see the Day approaching."*

This chapter will present five connection steps to maintain a connection with God. This can be compared to taking prescription medication for an illness. Medication is prescribed to treat the ailment so it does not grow worse. The ailment of a non-Christian is living a life apart from God, the Creator. Maintaining your connection with God will keep you spiritually strong.

MAINTAINING YOUR *GOD* CONNECTION

Connection 1
Find the Right Church and Become Planted
PSALM 92:12-14; EPHESIANS 4:11-16

The righteous shall flourish like a palm tree; he shall grow like a cedar in Lebanon. Those who are planted in the house of the Lord shall flourish in the courts of our God. They shall still bear fruit in old age; they shall be fresh and flourishing.

PSALM 92:12-14

Often times, individuals choose a church based upon their preferences and levels of comfort. A church should be chosen through the leading of the Holy Spirit. The church in which you become planted will be a place to serve as well as to be equipped to fulfill your God-ordained purpose. Such a church will uphold the standards of the Bible. If not, run!

*And He Himself gave some to be apostles, some prophets, some evangelists, and some pastors, and teachers, for the **equipping** of the saints, till we all come to the unity of the faith and of the knowledge of the Son of God, to a perfect (mature) man (mankind), to the measure of the stature of the fullness of Christ.*

EPHESIANS 4:12-13

The purpose of the church is to equip Christians to become spiritually mature to bring others to Christ and fulfill their God-ordained purpose. To be equipped is to have everything needed to achieve an intended goal or result. The ministry gifts (apostle, prophet, evangelist, pastor, and teacher) are for the equipping of the saints. These individuals are responsible for providing the saints (Christians) what is needed (teaching of the Word, correction, and advisement) to live victoriously in Christ. Verse 13 gives the result of being equipped. Being equipped will cause the saints to be 1) unified in the faith (in Christ), 2) knowledgeable of the Son of God (Christ), 3) a perfect (mature) Christian, and 4) to experience the fullness and completeness that comes with knowing Christ.

As a Christian it is your responsibility to become planted in the church God has chosen. Becoming planted can take on many different functions. For example, this includes working in a ministry area that best suits your gifts and abilities, leadership roles and much more. For the sake of this writing, only the foundational aspect of being planted will be addressed. ***The foundational action of becoming planted is to join a church and maintain consistent attendance at regularly scheduled services so that your spirit will receive spiritual nourishment from the Word of God.*** This is non-negotiable.

When an object is planted, it is stationary in one place getting the necessary nourishment to remain vital, healthy and strong. Psalm 1:3 says, *"He shall be like a tree* **planted** *by the rivers of water, that brings forth fruit in its season, whose leaf also shall not wither; and whatever he does shall prosper."* Becoming planted in a local church results in a vital, healthy, and strong relationship with Christ.

Questions and Answers

1. **What is the purpose of the church?**

   _____
   _____
   _____

2. **What does it mean to be *planted* in a church?**

   _____
   _____
   _____

3. **What are the results of becoming planted?**

   _____
   _____
   _____

How Do I Know When God Is Leading Me to Become Planted in a Church?

God desires that every Christian become planted in a local church. If you have not found a church or do not attend consistently, make a commitment to seek God regarding where you should become planted. The following are some questions to help determine where God desires for you to be planted. Place a "Y" for yes or "N" for no next to each question below.

1. Does the pastor or designee preach and teach messages that are in proper alignment with the Bible providing scriptural references so that you can study in your personal time? _____

2. Is there peace in your spirit when you attend? Is there peace in your spirit even if the sermon deals with personal situations that may be uncomfortable? _____

3. Do you receive specific strategies and solutions to personal situations in your life during the services? (This can include sermons, Sunday school/Bible study lessons, and prophetic sayings.) _____

4. Have you experienced positive results by acting upon the teachings and strategies taught during services? _____

5. Are you spiritually challenged to go beyond your present spiritual level? _____

If your answer is yes to all of the above stated questions, it is a good indication that God may be leading you to become planted in this specific church. You may need to consider other factors along with these questions. Remain prayerful and seek wise, godly counsel. God will always reveal and confirm His perfect will for you.

 Self-Check

1. Based upon the questions in the previous survey, assess where you are currently attending church. Have you chosen this church based upon your personal preferences and opinions, or where God is leading you?

   _____
   _____
   _____

2. Are you planted? What evidence do you see to prove your answer?

   _____
   _____
   _____

Connection 2
Remain Distraction Free
1 PETER 5:8-9

Be sober, be vigilant; because your adversary the devil walks about like a roaring lion, seeking whom he may devour. Resist him, steadfast in the faith, knowing that the same sufferings are experienced by your brotherhood in the world.

1 PETER 5:8-9

Many Christians allow distractions to pull them away from staying connected to the activities and people God has divinely appointed to help them in their Christian walk. These distractions can be jobs, friends, family, or even relationships. If people or things pose a distraction to your spiritual connection, remove them immediately.

 Self-Check

1. List people, relationships or things that are a distraction to your Christian faith.

   _____
   _____
   _____
   _____

2. What steps will you take to remove the distractions listed above?

   _____
   _____
   _____
   _____

3. List any distractions that may be difficult for you to remove on your own. Make a commitment to share with another mature Christian. This will provide support, instruction and accountability to remove these distractions.

   _____
   _____
   _____
   _____

Connection 3
Study of God's Word

A Christian should develop a consistent habit of reading and studying God's Word in addition to communing with God in prayer.

1. Study God's Word

(Psalm 119:105; John 1:1-5; Matthew 4:4; John 6:32-35; 1 Corinthians 10:3-4)

> *Be diligent to present yourself approved to God, a worker who does not need to be ashamed, rightly dividing the word of truth.* 2 TIMOTHY 2:15

- **Private Bible Study:** Private Bible study should *always* include the teachings and sermons taught at Sunday school or small group, Sunday worship service, and mid-week services. This includes ***finding, confessing, and meditating*** on Scripture that deal with a specific area to be improved. For example, if there is an issue with speaking negative about oneself or situations, a verse should be found that provides a resolve against negative talking. Ephesians 4:29 says, "*Let no corrupt word proceed out of your mouth, but what is good for necessary edification, that it may impart grace to the hearers.*" This is where a topical Bible, such as *Be Like Jesus Scriptures for Transformation*, will be very useful. It has the Scriptures listed by topics and categories, and it is a good companion to this curriculum.

- **Confessing God's Word:** The Bible says, *"You shall have what you say"* (paraphrase of Mark 11:23). Therefore, if certain situations are not reflecting the Word (Scripture), then you need to speak the Word until you see those situations change. Speaking the Word will also strengthen your faith to believe God for what is needed. *See Psalm 119:172; Proverbs 10:11; Mark 11:22-24; and Hebrews 4:14, 10:23.*

- **Meditating on God's Word:** To meditate means to mutter over and over; engage in thought or contemplation; reflect. Joshua 1:8 says, "*This Book of the Law shall not depart from your mouth, but you shall meditate in it day and night, that you may observe to do* *according to all that is written in it. Then you will make your way prosperous and then you will have good success."* Meditating is taking the time to focus solely on God's Word through thought and speech, getting it deep into the spirit. *See Psalm 77:12, 104:34, 119:23, 143:5; and 1 Timothy 4:13,15.*

Self-Check

1. **Assess your study time on a scale of 1-4 for the categories below.**
   (**1** – I do not engage; **2** – I engage 1-2 times/week; **3** – I engage 3-4 times/week; **4** – I engage 5 times or more/week)

   a) **Private Bible study:**

   b) **Confessing God's Word:**

   c) **Meditating on God's Word:**

2. **For the areas receiving a score of a 1 or 2, develop and write out weekly goals to achieve a level 3 or 4 engagement score. Use the space below to develop and write your goals. Refer to the "Suggested Prayer and Study Practices," at the end of this chapter for suggestions of how to begin.**

   _____
   _____
   _____
   _____
   _____

Connection 4
Prayer: Dialogue with God

PSALM 5:3, 40:1; JEREMIAH 23:23;
MATTHEW 18:19-20; HEBREWS 4:16; 1 JOHN 5:14-15

1. **Two-Way Conversation:** Prayer does not only consist of the Christian talking to God. God also wants to talk to you. Do not get locked into a one-way conversation.

2. **Learning God's Voice:** In general, God will speak through the conscience (thoughts), which is the voice of the human spirit. Have you ever had a thought that something just was not right or that you should do something at a particular time? That is God speaking through your human spirit. By feeding your spirit the Word of God, it will be trained to hear the voice of God. John 10:4 states, *"And the sheep follow him, for they know his voice."* In this passage, Christians are referred to as sheep. Sheep follow the shepherd, which is God. Learning to recognize God's voice is powerful. He will begin to speak in a more detailed and intimate manner. Keeping a pure mind and spirit, maintaining a godly atmosphere, and consistency in the Word and prayer guarantee open dialogue with God.

 Self-Check

1. **How often do you pray? Assess your prayer time on a scale of 1-4.**
   (**1** – I do not engage; **2** – I engage 1-2 times/week; **3** – I engage 3-4 times/week; **4** – I engage 5 times or more/week)

2. **If your engagement score is a 1 or 2, develop and write out weekly goals to achieve a level 3 or 4 engagement score. Use the space below to develop and write your goals. Refer to the "Suggested Prayer and Study Practices," at the end of this chapter for suggestions of how to begin.**

   _____
   _____
   _____
   _____
   _____

Connection 5
Fellowship with Other Christians
ACTS 2:42-43, 46-47; HEBREWS 10:24-25

And let us consider one another in order to stir up love and good works, not forsaking the assembling of ourselves together, as is the manner of some, but exhorting one another, and so much the more as you see the Day approaching.

HEBREWS 10:24-25

The Bible clearly states that Christians are to fellowship with other Christians to remain encouraged and strengthened. This was evident in the early church in the book of Acts (Acts 2:42). They were always fellowshipping and strengthening themselves in their newfound faith. Christianity was a new faith, and often times Christians were persecuted simply for believing in Christ. They consistently strengthened and encouraged one another so that the possibility of persecution would not cause them to turn from Christ. Make it a priority to attend church-sponsored fellowships, outings, and church services. This will provide opportunities to be around other strong Christians.

Self-Check

1. **Evaluate the company you keep. Do these individuals encourage you to maintain your relationship with the Lord and obedience to His word?**

___
___
___
___
___

Suggested Prayer and Study Practices

Every Christian needs to have uninterrupted time with God. Below is a suggested outline of how to develop a habit of one-on-one time with God.

First Fruits – Beginning the Day

- **Praise and Thanksgiving - 15 minutes**

  This is time when you simply thank God for who He is and for the blessings He has bestowed upon your life. You can include Scripture verses of praise. The book of Psalms is a great place to start. You can also praise God in the Holy Spirit (tongues). Refer to chapter 5 "The Holy Spirit" for an in-depth explanation.

- **Reading and Meditating on Scripture - 15 minutes**

  God may lay a particular Scripture on your heart, or you can refer to verses on a specific area you are dealing with. You can also refer to verses from the sermon at previous services.

- **Proclamations to "Speak Over Your Day" – 1-2 Minutes**

  Take a few moments to command your day. You tell the day what it is going to be.

  Examples include, but are not limited to:
  This day will be successful and productive.
  I will walk in the favor of God.
  I will progress and prosper in all things today.
  My body is healed, and I am strong.

  Scriptural proclamations:
  I am the head and not the tail (DEUTERONOMY 28:13).
  No weapon formed against me shall prosper (ISAIAH 54:17).
  I can do all things through Christ that strengthens me (PHILIPPIANS 4:13).
  My God shall supply all of my needs according to His riches in glory (PHILIPPIANS 4:20).

Necessary Study Tools for All Christians

Study Bible

Obtain a study Bible in a version you can understand. The New King James Version, The Amplified Bible, and The New Living Translation Bible are versions that are easy to understand. A study Bible will have a commentary section that will explain the proper interpretations of the Scripture passages you are reading.

Topical Bible or Bible Promise Book

This is a Bible that is organized by topic. For example, if the issue is anger, it will list verses on that topic. The title may be Topical Bible or Promise Book; however, they serve the same purpose. *Be Like Jesus Scriptures for Transformation* is highly recommended.

Concordance

A concordance lists Scripture based upon key words. The verse, "I can do all things through Christ that gives me strength," can be found by looking up ***strength***. It will list the book and verse where it can be found in the Bible. There will also be other verses that include the word ***strength***. If Scripture verses for a particular word or topic are needed, the concordance will list all the verses accordingly. For example, if verses for ***salvation*** are needed, the concordance will list all those that have the word ***salvation*** in them.

*A local or online Christian bookstore retailer can assist with locating these items.

CHAPTER 3

Maintaining Salvation

MAINTAINING SALVATION

Hallelujah! You have taken the initial step of receiving salvation by believing, confessing, and making Jesus Christ Lord. From this point forward, it is vital that you maintain your free gift of salvation.

WHY MUST I MAINTAIN A FREE GIFT?

Christianity is a lifestyle rooted in love through a relationship with Jesus Christ. As noted in chapter 1, salvation is everlasting (perpetual, enduring) in nature. It is a continual process in the life of a Christian beyond initial conversion. The perpetual nature of salvation is manifested through a relationship with Christ. Love is what caused Jesus to go to the cross to bear our sins. Love always gives back. It should not be burdensome to live according to God's commandments (John 14:15; 1 John 5:3). A Christian lifestyle requires one to develop a mentality and perspective that is based from the Word of God and cultivated through the spirit of God (Philippians 2:5). John 15:4 states, *"Abide in Me, and I in you. As the branch cannot bear fruit of itself, unless it abides in the vine, neither can you, unless you abide in Me."*

To maintain something is to keep in existence preserving from decline. To maintain something, it first must be received. When you received Jesus Christ as your personal Savior, you received salvation. Again, salvation is **deliverance** and **preservation** from sin, illusion, and destruction, restoring to a better state of existence. Salvation is a free gift. It cannot be earned, nor obtained through works. If salvation is to remain in perpetual existence as God intended, the Christian lifestyle (relationship with God) must be maintained through prayer, study, attending church, and other activities as stated in the "Seven Steps to Maintaining Salvation" section located at the end of this chapter.

Receiving Salvation

- One believes and confesses Jesus Christ.
- Jesus Christ is Lord (sole authority) in a Christian's life.
- Salvation is freely given and does not have to be earned.

Maintaining Salvation

Nurturing the gift of salvation so that the gift remains in perpetual (continuous) existence through:

- Getting planted in a local church
- Prayer and Bible study
- Maintaining a godly atmosphere

Practical Example

If someone were to give me a car, I would be ecstatic! This would mean no debt! Though the car was given to me free and clear, it does not dismiss the reality that I will need to maintain the servicing of the car. First, I need to keep gas in the car so that I can get to my destinations. Second, a car needs oil and fluid changes, tire rotations and balances, and additional services required to maintain performance. If I do not maintain the service requirements for my free car it will not perform at its maximum potential. Its life span will decline quickly, ultimately resulting in loss. Salvation is the car without debt. The giver of the car is Jesus Christ. A relationship with Jesus Christ is the gas. It keeps everything moving. The servicing of the car is consistent prayer, study of God's Word, and getting planted in a local church.

If I want my car to perform at its best I am going to make sure I acquire the best maintenance. I am going to fill up the car with a high quality grade of gas to ensure maximum performance. My relationship with God is high grade. I intentionally make time for God both privately and corporately (church). I may have to get up a bit earlier to give Him the first part of my day. I guard my time with the Lord by eliminating all distractions. When it is time for my car to be serviced, I do not procrastinate, nor become neglectful. When I take my car to be serviced I want honest and skillful mechanics that are knowledgeable of my particular vehicle and can provide the service and proper recommendations.

I maintain my spiritual servicing by attending church each week and engaging in personal Bible study and prayer. My pastor (mechanic) knows my spiritual needs because it is the church where God has planted me. I am exposed to truth and fresh spiritual perspectives from God that provides new and deeper insight into the Scriptures. I also receive confirmation in regards to what God has shared with me in my personal time. My intentional efforts to give God my best and to get the best spiritual nourishment move me from a state of religion to relationship. Therefore, Christianity becomes a lifestyle geared towards an intimate relationship with Jesus Christ.

Work It Out

I want to provide a scriptural reference for the practical example from Philippians 2:12-13.

> *Work out your own salvation with fear and trembling; for it is God who works in you both to will and to do for His good pleasure* (New King James Version).

> *Work hard to show the results of your salvation, obeying God with deep reverence and fear. For God is working in you, giving you the desire and the power to do what pleases him* (New Living Translation).

Two different translations were used because I want to bring clarity to what the Apostle Paul was implying with the word *work*. The phrase *work out* as stated in the New King James Version originates from the Greek word *Katergazomai* meaning "to do that from which something results of things: bring about, result in."[3]

The word *work* in the context of this Scripture does not indicate that salvation is obtained through merited works. *Work* is used in the context of intentional effort. An intentional effort to nurture and maintain your gift of salvation brings about or results in the manifestation of salvation on a continual basis in the life of a Christian.

Questions and Answers

1. What is the difference between receiving salvation and maintaining salvation?

   _____
   _____
   _____

2. Philippians 2:12-13 (NLT) says, _____ _____ to show the _____ of your _____, _____ God with _____ and _____. For God is _____ in you _____ you the _____ and the _____ to _____ what _____ _____.

3. Explain what *work out* means in Philippians 2:12-13.

   _____
   _____
   _____

 Self-Check

4. **What areas in your life are you working on so that it reflects the results of salvation? Include how you are working.**

   Example 1 – Finances: budgeting, saving, debt elimination
   a. Budgeting – Get samples of a budget and create one using current income and expenditures.
   b. Saving – Eliminate unnecessary spending based on the budget and place those funds into a savings account.
   c. Debt Elimination – Make a list of all debts including pay off balances. Include in budget.

   Example 2 – Addiction
   a. The root of addiction is rebellion. Make an assessment to evaluate where obedience to God has not been active.
   b. Remove people, places, and things that contribute to the addiction or serve as triggers.
   c. Attend a church that teaches the uncompromised Word of God and get planted.
   d. Find someone that will provide accountability.

   _____
   _____
   _____
   _____
   _____
   _____

CHRISTIANS AND SINNERS

The Christian lifestyle must be governed according to the Bible. Those who *consistently* engage in lifestyles and activities that do not align with the standards of the Bible cannot profess they are truly Christian.

> *Not everyone who says to Me, "Lord, Lord," shall enter the kingdom of heaven, but he who does the will of My Father in heaven.* MATTHEW 7:21

The title Christian was given to the disciples of Jesus in the city of Antioch as stated in Acts 11:26. Christian is derived from the Greek word *Christianos* meaning a follower of Christ.[4] Therefore, a Christian is one who believes in the Father, Son, and Holy Spirit; has received salvation; and displays behavior that reflects the godly standards set forth in the Bible. The title of sinner refers to one who consistently engages in sinful behavior. Sin is behavior that contradicts the Word of God.

What is the difference between those who live a life of sin and a Christian who happens to sin? Individuals who live a life of sin are sinners because they consistently engage in a sinful lifestyle. A true Christian is not a sinner because they do not consistently engage in a sinful lifestyle. Therefore, the phrase "I am a sinner saved by grace" is incorrect. It should be stated, "I was a sinner; now I am saved by grace."

> *What shall we say then? Shall we continue in sin that grace may abound? Certainly not! How shall we who died to sin live any longer in it?* ROMANS 6:1-2

If a Christian happens to sin, it is appropriate to ask for forgiveness and repent. It does not mean that person is no longer saved. Forgiveness does not release the Christian from the responsibility of working on his or her weak areas. It is a command for Christians to work out their soul salvation with fear and trembling (Philippians 2:12-13). If a sinner desires to become a Christian, he or she must receive salvation as stated in chapter 1. Read the additional Scriptures taken from the Amplified Bible. These specific verses provide clarity and insight regarding the difference between a Christian and a sinner.

- *And when Jesus heard it, He said to them, Those who are strong and well have no need of a physician, but those who are weak and sick; I came not to call the righteous ones to repentance, but sinners (the erring ones and all those not free from sin).*

    MARK 2:17

- *But I say, walk and live [habitually] in the [Holy] Spirit [responsive to and controlled and guided by the Spirit]; then you will certainly not gratify the cravings and desires of the flesh (of human nature without God). For the desires of the flesh are opposed to the [Holy] Spirit, and the [desires of the] Spirit are opposed to the flesh (godless human nature); for these are antagonistic to each other [continually withstanding and in conflict with each other], so that you are not free but are prevented from doing what you desire to do. But if you are guided (led) by the [Holy] Spirit, you are not subject to the Law.*

    Now the doings (practices) of the flesh are clear (obvious): they are immorality, impurity, indecency, idolatry, sorcery, enmity, strife, jealousy, anger (ill temper), selfishness, divisions (dissensions), party spirit (factions, sects with peculiar opinions, heresies), envy, drunkenness, carousing, and the like. I warn you beforehand, just as I did previously, that those who do such things shall not inherit the kingdom of God.

    But the fruit of the [Holy] Spirit [the work which His presence within accomplishes] is love, joy (gladness), peace, patience (an even temper, forbearance), kindness, goodness (benevolence), faithfulness, gentleness (meekness, humility), self-control (self-restraint, continence). Against such things there is no law [that can bring a charge].

    And those who belong to Christ Jesus (the Messiah) have crucified the flesh (the godless human nature) with its passions and appetites and desires. If we live by the [Holy] Spirit, let us also walk by the Spirit. [If by the Holy Spirit we have our life in God, let us go forward walking in line, our conduct controlled by the Spirit.].

    GALATIANS 5:16-25

- *But as He who called you is holy, you also be holy in all your conduct, because it is written, "Be holy, for I am holy."*
  1 PETER 1:15-16

- *Now, "If the righteous one is scarcely saved, where will the ungodly and the sinner appear?"*
  1 PETER 4:18

- *No one who abides in Him [who lives and remains in communion with and in obedience to Him—deliberately, knowingly and habitually] commits (practices) sin. No one who [habitually] sins has either seen or known Him [recognized, perceived or understood Him, or has had an experiential acquaintance with Him].*

  Boys (lads), let no one deceive and lead you astray. He who practices righteousness [who is upright, conforming to the divine will in purpose, thought and action, living a consistently conscientious life] is righteous, even as He is righteous.

  [But] he who commits sin [who practices evildoing] is of the devil [takes his character from the evil one], for the devil has sinned (violated the divine law) from the beginning. The reason the Son of God was made manifest (visible) was to undo (destroy, loosen and dissolve) the works the devil [has done].

  *No one born (begotten) of God [deliberately, knowingly and habitually] practices sin, for God's nature abides in him [His principle of life, the divine **seed**, remains permanently within him]; and he cannot practice sinning because he is born (begotten) of God.*

  By this it is made clear who take their nature from God and are His children and who take their nature from the devil and are his children: no one who does not practice righteousness [who does not conform to God's will in purpose, thought and action] is of God; neither is anyone who does not love his brother (his fellow believer in Christ).
  1 JOHN 3:6-10, V. 9 EMPHASIS ADDED

- *For the [true] love of God is this: that we do His commands [keep His ordinances and are mindful of His precepts and teaching]. And these orders of His are not irksome (burdensome, oppressive or grievous).* 1 JOHN 5:3

- *All wrongdoing is sin, and there is sin which does not [involve] death [that may be repented of and forgiven].* 1 JOHN 5:17

Questions and Answers

1. **What is the difference between a Christian and a sinner?**

2. **Why is the phrase "I am a sinner saved by grace" incorrect?**

3. **List at least two Scriptures that prove an individual cannot be both a Christian and a sinner.**

Self-Check

4. Assess your lifestyle. Based upon the verses listed in this section, are you a Christian or a sinner?

5. Using the answer you provided in the previous question, list at least two actions in which you consistently engage to prove your answer to be an accurate assessment. What Scripture verses can you find to prove that the actions you listed are those of a Christian or a sinner?

REPENTANCE

1 John 1:9 says, *"If we confess our sins, He is faithful and just to forgive us our sins and to cleanse us from all unrighteousness."* Once sin has been confessed, and forgiveness has been obtained, repentance must be put into action. Before we go any further with repentance, let us review forgiveness.

Forgiveness grants release from payment or indebtedness. When Jesus stated that *"He is faithful and just to forgive us our sins"* (1 John 1:9), it means that our sins are not held against us. He has wiped the slate clean. Hallelujah! Once forgiveness is obtained, a conscious decision must be made to no longer sin. Christians are to live a life of repentance. We should always stay in a mode of making decisions to follow Christ.

Repentance is a 1) **changed mind to do the will of God** 2) **accompanied with the appropriate actions** (actions that are aligned with the Word of God) (Romans 12:1-2). Mark 2:17 says, *"Those who are well have no need of a physician, but those who are sick. I did not come to call the righteous, but sinners, to repentance."* In this passage of Scripture, Jesus is making the point that the righteous (those in right relationship with Him) do not need to repent. They have already turned away from sin and are now in proper relationship with God. It is the sinner He is calling to repentance. Below is a concise explanation of forgiveness and repentance.

> *Forgiveness* is God's responsibility. All one has to do is ask and receive.

> *Repentance* is the individual's responsibility to change their mindset to do the will of God *accompanied with appropriate actions*.

Read this example of repentance:

> *Hi, my name is Todd. Before I received salvation I had a bad habit of using profanity, especially when I became angry. I immediately asked God for forgiveness in this area but still struggled with using profanity. When I learned of repentance in my Christian Living class at church, I learned that I had to do more than just ask for forgiveness. I learned that I can receive forgiveness when I ask, but I had to put actions in place and*

make a decision to turn away from sin. I learned that repentance is a changed mind to do the will of God accompanied with the appropriate actions. I found Scripture verses that specifically dealt with godly communication. Ephesians 4:29 is one of my favorites! Studying and confessing these Scriptures helped me change my mindset about profanity and adopt godly communication.

Second, I made a decision to ask my friends and coworkers not to use profanity in my presence. I also eliminated music, television shows, and movies that contained profanity. I noticed after a few weeks I was no longer using profanity.

Using the Scriptures to change my mind and putting a plan into action helped me achieve true deliverance. I now notice that I am able to edify and encourage others in the way of the Lord. To God be all the glory!

This short story illustrates the changes Todd made in his life to ensure that he would not fall back into the ungodly behavior of using profanity. God does not forgive with the intention that we return to sinful behavior.

Let's review Todd's process of deliverance. Again, repentance is **a changed mind to do the will of God with appropriate actions**.

1. Todd stated that he attended his Christian Living class. It is vitally important that Christians stay connected to God through personal prayer, study time, and becoming planted in a local church. This cannot be stated enough! Todd consistently attended church.

2. Second, Todd changed his mindset about profanity by using the Word of God. He found Scripture verses for his specific problem. When going through the process of deliverance, it is vitally important to find verses that edify your spirit to do the opposite of the behavior that is not glorifying God. In this case, Todd needed to adopt godly communication; therefore, he found verses pertaining to this area.

3. Third, Todd had to take some action to stop exposing himself to profanity. This resulted in changing conversation styles and entertainment choices. When changing your lifestyle, it is also important to acknowledge when it is necessary to change the company you keep. This may involve releasing some friends, family, and other relationships. If a relationship is pushing you away from God, then it is time to make a change.

4. Last, Todd was able to be a witness to encourage and edify others in the way of the Lord. Always remember that repentance has two parts: 1) a ***changed mind*** to obey the Word of God with 2) ***appropriate actions*** (actions that match your decision to obey the Word of God). Mark 2:17 proves that you cannot be saved and continue to sin. Living a life of sin takes you out of right relationship (righteousness) with God. Once you are out of relationship you have lost your place in the kingdom of God. Repentance is necessary to restore a right relationship with God, as well as restoration to your rightful place in the kingdom of God (Luke 15:11-31). This puts to rest the incorrect belief of "once saved, always saved" (1 Peter 4:18). Scripture does not prove that doctrine to be accurate. Repentance shows gratitude to God for the gift of salvation and forgiveness given to us, which we do not deserve on our own merit (Luke 15:19-31).

And when Jesus heard it, He said to them, Those who are strong and well have no need of a physician, but those who are weak and sick; I came not to call the righteous ones to repentance, but sinners (the erring ones and all those not free from sin).

MARK 2:17(AMP)

For the kind of sorrow God wants us to experience leads us away from sin and results in salvation. There's no regret for that kind of sorrow. But worldly sorrow, which lacks repentance, results in spiritual death.

2 CORINTHIANS 7:10

Questions and Answers

1. List the two parts of repentance:

   a. _____

   accompanied with

   b. _____

2. What Scriptures support the actions of repentance?

   _____

   _____

3. What is the difference between forgiveness and repentance?

   _____

   _____

4. What did Todd do to get a "changed mind to do the will of God" (the first part of repentance)?

   _____

   _____

5. What actions did Todd display with the second part of repentance (accompanying actions)?

   _____

   _____

 Self-Check

6. **Identify areas in your life in which you need to exemplify repentance. For each area list the following:**

   a) **Changed Mind** – Find Scriptures that address your area of need (a topical Bible will help with this). Remember that you need to do the opposite of the sin. Find verses that support the behavior or goal you are striving to achieve.
   Example - Anger, Ephesians 4:26

   b) **Accompanying actions to support a changed mind** – List the actions that need to be implemented to facilitate a full repentance.
   Example - Anger: 1) Stop and count to ten. 2) Pray before responding. 3) Discontinue spending time with people who trigger the anger.

WHAT IS GRACE?

Grace is unmerited supernatural assistance given to humans for their regeneration (a life reflecting the fruit of salvation) and sanctification (set apart for holiness). Unmerited means it was given without having to be earned. Pastor Dennis Clark offers an excellent definition of grace:

> *Grace is the personal presence of Jesus enabling and empowering Christians to be and to do ALL that He called you to be and ALL that He called you to do.*[5]

Grace does not excuse sin but empowers the Christian to come out of sin, repent and bear godly fruit.

> *For by **grace** you have been saved through faith, and that not of yourselves; it is the gift of God, not of works, lest anyone should boast. For we are His workmanship, created in Christ Jesus for **good works**, which God prepared beforehand that we should walk in them.* EPHESIANS 2:8-10

Christians are saved by God's grace and not by works or actions. In other words, we cannot do anything to earn salvation. It has been freely given; therefore, we are to receive freely. Ephesians 2:8-10 states that a person's works (actions and behaviors) cannot save; however, it does not excuse the requirement that a Christian should exemplify Christ-like behavior. In Ephesians 2:10, Paul states, *"We are His workmanship, created in Christ Jesus for good works which God prepared beforehand that we should walk in them."* This proves that grace is given to supernaturally assist a Christian to obey the commandments of Christ displaying good works (godly actions and behavior).

Questions and Answers

1. What is grace?

    Grace is the _____ _____ of Jesus _____ and _____ Christians to _____ and to _____ ALL that He _____ you to _____ and ALL that He _____ you to _____.

2. What was your understanding of grace prior to this study?

    _____
    _____
    _____

✓ Self-Check

3. Describe what *grace* should look like in your life as a Christian.

    _____
    _____
    _____
    _____

FASTING

This section will provide answers to frequently asked questions about fasting. Fasting is a biblical practice that produces a greater depth of intimacy with God, which manifests beneficial results. The practice of fasting may be uncomfortable but it assists a Christian to attain and maintain the results of salvation (deliverance and preservation).

What is fasting?
Fasting is abstaining from food for a specific amount of time.

What is the purpose of fasting?
Fasting develops a closer, stronger, and more intimate relationship with God.

How does fasting strengthen a relationship with God?
1. Fasting holistically humbles one (spirit, soul, and body) before God (*Psalm 35:13*).
2. Fasting empties oneself to be refilled with God (*John 3:30-31*).
3. Fasting re-centers the relationship with God (*Proverbs 3:5-6*).
4. Fasting chastens (corrects) bringing one into complete obedience (*Psalm 69:10; Romans 8:5*).
5. Fasting crucifies the appetite creating a dependence on God (*Galatians 5:24*).

What are the results of fasting?
1. Undistracted earnestness (seriousness) towards God both during and after fasting (*Luke 9:23; 1 Corinthians 7:5*)
2. Obedience (*Isaiah 58:6*)
3. Victory over temptation, addiction, and oppression (*Luke 4: 1-13*)
4. Power over demonic spirits (*Matthew 17:14-21*)
5. Develops faith and crucifies unbelief (doubt) (*Matthew 17:19-21*)
6. Empowers prayer (*Matthew 4:1-11, 17:14-21*)
7. Physical healing (*Isaiah 58:8*)

When should a Christian fast?
1. When prompted by the Holy Spirit (*Isaiah 58:6*)
2. In need (*Ezra 8:21*)
3. Danger (*Esther 4*)
4. Worried (*Daniel 6:18-23*)
5. In trouble (*Acts 27:9, 33*)
6. Spiritual conflict (*Matthew 4:1-11*)
7. Desperate in prayer (*Acts 9*)

Types of Fast
1. Liquid Fast
2. Vegetarian Fast – Abstinence of animal, artificially flavored, and processed foods.
3. Individual Meal Fast – Abstinence from specific meals (breakfast, lunch, or dinner).

Fasting and Praying
Fasting should always be accompanied with prayer. Fasting requires dependence on God to endure. Maintaining a strong prayer life when fasting strengthens the connection with God; therefore, strengthening faith. This guarantees that God will provide whatever is needed to endure the time of fasting. It is the element of prayer coupled with fasting that brings about supernatural results. Fasting without prayer is nothing more than abstaining from food. *See Matthew 17:14-21.*

Fasting with a Pure Motive
Fasting should be done privately. It should not be done to flaunt how spiritual or dedicated one is to God. It should earnestly be done so that God receives the glory by the fruit it bears in the life of a Christian. *See Matthew 6:16-18 and Luke 18:11-13.*

Fasting Best Practices
There are some practices that should be exemplified to obtain the best results from the fasting period. These practices will eliminate distractions so that one can give complete attention to the Lord.

1. Eliminate entertainment, including TV, music, gaming devices, shopping, movies, or anything that serves the purpose of entertaining. This best practice should be observed both at home and in motor vehicles. This time can be spent in prayer, meditation, or study. Electronic devices such as an iPod or mp3 player are recommended to listen to audio versions of the Bible/Scriptures and sermons or teachings.
2. Eliminate the use of cell phones and any other handheld device unless it is for work or to keep in touch with family in the event of an emergency.
3. Refrain from social media unless it is required for work purposes.
4. Incorporate family Bible study if this is not already in practice.
5. Refrain from eating out if you are on a modified meal fast. It eliminates distractions, temptations, and exposure to carnal entertainment. This is a great opportunity to learn how to prepare healthy entrees to maintain ultimate health for the work of the Kingdom.
6. If possible, turn off your electronic devices during prayer and study time. If this is not possible for work or family reasons, set up special rings or alerts to receive important calls.
7. See the following Scriptures to help maintain focus on God: *Psalm 119:1-3; Proverbs 5:1-2; Isaiah 50:7, 58:1-14; Philippians 4:8; 1 Peter 5:8.*

Questions and Answers

1. State the purpose of fasting in your own words.

2. List at least three of the five ways fasting strengthens a relationship with God.

3. List at least four of the seven results of fasting.

4. List four of the seven occasions in which a Christian should fast.

5. Why is prayer necessary during fasting?

6. List four of the seven Fasting Best Practices.

 Self-Check

7. Assess your previous fasting experiences. Did you experience any of the results listed in this section? How so?

   _____

   _____

   _____

   _____

8. What Fasting Best Practices will you implement on your next fast that you have not previously done?

   _____

   _____

   _____

   _____

WHAT IF I STILL HAVE ISSUES AFTER I BECOME A CHRISTIAN?

All Christians will have areas in their lives in which they may struggle. No one should ever be ashamed of having issues. Grace empowers the Christian to overcome every struggle and issue in life. Are your issues defeating you? Philippians 2:12-13 states, *"Work out your own salvation with fear and trembling; for it is God who works in you both to will and to do for His good pleasure."* The following are some questions to help determine if you are **working out your soul salvation**. Place a "Y" for yes or "N" for no next to each question below.

- Have you made up your mind to live like a Christian? _____
- Have you submitted your issues to the Lord? _____
- Do you have **corresponding actions** that will bring about deliverance in the area(s) in which you are experiencing difficulty? _____
- Are you actively engaged in the Word finding verses to address your issues? _____
- Do you have other strong Christians holding you accountable? _____
- Are you planted and consistently attending a church that is teaching the uncompromised Word of God? _____

If the answer is yes to these questions, salvation is being worked out. If some or all of the answers were no, make the necessary steps to activate the actions in the questions so that those answers become yes. God knows His children will have issues. That is why He said in Hebrews 4:16, *"Let us therefore come boldly to the throne of grace, that we may obtain mercy and find grace to help in time of need."* Remember that you are saved by grace. This supernatural grace enables and empowers you to be what God has called you to be and do what He has commanded. You can overcome your issues! To activate this grace (the personal presence of Jesus), you have to feed and maintain your spirit with the Word of God. Refer to "The Seven Steps to Maintaining Salvation" at the end of this chapter for more detail.

A relationship with Christ has to be maintained. In other words, what you say and what you do must match. This is proven in the following Scriptures taken from the New King James Version:

> *"Not everyone who says to Me, 'Lord, Lord,' shall enter the kingdom of heaven, but he who does the will of My Father in heaven. Many will say to Me in that day, 'Lord, Lord, have we not prophesied in Your name, cast out demons in Your name, and done many wonders in Your name?' And then I will declare to them, 'I never knew you; depart from Me, you who practice lawlessness!'"* MATTHEW 7:21-23

> *Well then, should we keep on sinning so that God can show us more and more of his wonderful grace? Of course not! Since we have died to sin, how can we continue to live in it? Or have you forgotten that when we were joined with Christ Jesus in baptism we joined him in his death? For we died and were buried with Christ by baptism. And just as Christ was raised from the dead by the glorious power of the Father, now we also may live new lives . . . Well then, since God's grace has set us free from the law, does that mean we can go on sinning? Of course not!* ROMANS 6:1-4, 15, NLT

> *Therefore, if anyone is in Christ, he is a new creation; old things have passed away; behold, all things have become new.* 2 CORINTHIANS 5:17

> *Do not be unequally yoked together with unbelievers. For what fellowship has righteousness with lawlessness? And what communion has light with darkness? And what accord has Christ with Belial? Or what part has a believer with an unbeliever? And what agreement has the temple of God with idols? For you are the temple of the living God. As God has said, "I will dwell in them and walk among them. I will be their God, and they shall be My people." Therefore, "Come out from among them and be separate," says the Lord. "Do not touch what is unclean, and I will receive you. I will be a Father to you, and you shall be My sons and daughters," says the Lord Almighty.* 2 CORINTHIANS 6:14-18

Therefore, my beloved, as you have always obeyed, not as in my presence only, but now much more in my absence, work out your own salvation with fear and trembling; for it is God who works in you both to will and to do for His good pleasure.

PHILIPPIANS 2:12-13

But as He who called you is holy, you also be holy in all your conduct, because it is written, "Be holy, for I am holy."   1 PETER 1:15-16

Now, "If the righteous one is scarcely saved, where will the ungodly and the sinner appear?"

1 PETER 4:18

Self-Check

1. **Select at least three Scriptures that support the maintaining of salvation.**

2. **Explain why you chose those particular verses.**

SEVEN STEPS TO MAINTAIN SALVATION

Listed below are seven steps, if consistently implemented, will help you to maintain your salvation.

Step 1
Get planted in a Bible-based, Holy Spirit-filled church (Psalm 92:12-14). This is the most critical step after receiving salvation. Getting planted in an uncompromising Word-based church will provide accountability and teaching of the Word of God. Attending church provides the opportunity to be around other Christians. The pastor or spiritual leader of a congregation watches for the souls of the parishioners, challenges their spiritual growth, and creates opportunities to develop gifts and talents. It is also essential not to allow situations or individuals to create a hindrance to your church connection.

Step 2
Read the Bible and pray every day (Matthew 4:4; Hebrews 4:16). Begin by studying and reviewing the sermons and teachings taught during Sunday worship, Bible study, Sunday school, and/or small group. Take an assessment of the areas that present difficulties. This could be finances, addiction, hanging around the wrong people, lying, cursing, laziness, or any other issue. Find Scriptures that address those areas and confess them daily until godly results are evident. A study Bible and topical Bible should be acquired to assist in effective study habits.

Step 3
Hang around other strong Christians (Hebrews 10:24-25). Make it a habit to be surrounded by other victorious Christians that will provide encouragement, strength, and accountability.

Step 4

Maintain a godly atmosphere (2 Corinthians 6:14). Prohibit anything that does not bring glory to God from entering the eye and ear gates. This includes music, movies, and television programs that glorify sinful behavior. Sinful behavior can be any actions that contradict the Word of God. In addition, do not become fearful to separate from individuals who are consistently negative and distract from the things of God.

Step 5

Get filled with the Holy Spirit (Acts 2:4). The Holy Spirit is the Spirit of God living inside every believer. The Holy Spirit is the third person of the Trinity and is the power source for the Christian. What separates Christianity from other religions is that Christians can have the power of the true and living God residing within. The power of the Holy Spirit gives us the supernatural ability to live victoriously in Christ and take authority over the flesh. Every Christian should desire to be filled with the Holy Spirit (also referred to as the baptism of the Holy Spirit). The Holy Spirit is given by simply asking to be filled. The evidence that one has received the infilling of the Holy Spirit is a heavenly utterance, commonly known as tongues. Refer to Acts 2 when the disciples were filled with the Holy Spirit. Chapter 5 explains the Holy Spirit in detail.

Step 6

Walk in the fruit of the Spirit (Galatians 5:16-26). The fruit of the Spirit has to do with Christian character. Salvation is for the whole person: spirit, soul, and body. Christians should walk in integrity displaying godly character. There are nine characteristics and manifestations of the fruit of the Spirit: love, joy, peace, patience, kindness, goodness, faithfulness, gentleness, and self-control.

Step 7

Witness. Jesus gives the disciples a command in Mark 16:15 to "preach the gospel to every creature." This is the great commission of the church of Jesus Christ. Christians are to tell others about the saving grace of Jesus Christ. The behavior and character of Christians should be the first witness. Second, Christians should engage in witnessing as the Holy Spirit dictates. This can be done through praying for others, sharing your testimony, encouraging and edifying through Scripture, and compelling others to come to Christ. Incorporate evangelism into your prayer life. Ask God to send you to individuals who need to hear about Christ.

Questions and Answers

1. **Review the "Seven Steps to Maintain Salvation." List the steps that are inactive in your life and what you will do to make them active.**

   _____
   _____
   _____
   _____
   _____
   _____
   _____
   _____

Chapter 4

The Trinity: Father, Son, and Holy Spirit

THE TRINITY:
FATHER, SON, AND HOLY SPIRIT

In the "Seven Steps to Maintain Salvation" in chapter 3, step 5 states that getting filled with the Holy Spirit will help a Christian maintain salvation. It is vital for every Christian to understand the Holy Spirit. He is the source for living victoriously in the Christian faith. The Holy Spirit is also referred to as the power source. Acts 1:8 says, *"But you shall receive power when the Holy Spirit has come upon you."* To gain a clear understanding of the function of the Holy Spirit, it is necessary to understand the Godhead (Father, Son, and Holy Spirit). This chapter is dedicated to explaining God our Father, His Son Jesus Christ, and the Holy Spirit.

The Trinity is comprised of the Father, the Son, and the Holy Spirit. They are all three distinct persons, with three distinct functions; yet they are one God (Isaiah 43:10, 44:6, 45:14, 18, 21-22). They are co-equal, co-eternal, and co-powerful. It is argued that the Trinity is not biblical because the actual word *trinity* is not in the Bible. Trinity is derived from the Latin word *trinitas* which is translated as "the number three or triad".[6]

The Trinity is best explained using the example of a family unit. In a family, there is a father, a mother, and usually at least one child. They are one family but have different functions: Robert Jones (father, husband), Sarah Jones (wife, mother), Chad Jones (son, brother), Tracy Jones (daughter, sister). They all come from the same family but are one family unit. It is the same with the Trinity. All three are a family unit that comes out of the source of God. God is the family unit: 1) God the Father: the creator and the source of everything. 2) God the Son (Jesus): Jesus comes from God and is the mediator between God and mankind. We are made righteous through Him. 3) God the Holy Spirit: the Spirit of God that lives on the inside of a Christian. He is the element that empowers Christians to carry out the mission of the church.

If each person of the Trinity were named according to societal norm for first and last names, they would be named as such: the God family: Father (first name) God (last name), Jesus God (the Son of God), Holy Spirit God. Three functions, but one family unit.

Another example would be a grocery store chain. For the sake of this example the chain is Manna Bread Grocery. Manna Bread Grocery is the corporation, but stores are located in various places. Though there may be various locations they are separate entities bearing the name Manna Bread Grocery. Each store serves its function where it is located—one entity with many locations.

Function of Each Person of the Trinity

This section will explain the designated purpose of the Father, the Son, and the Holy Spirit.

1. **The Function of the Father**

    Everything is sent out through the Father. He is the creator of everything. *See Genesis 1:1, 26 and Isaiah 42:5, 45:18.*

2. **The Function of the Son**

    The Son (Jesus Christ) is the receiver of the Father's authority and the mediator between God and man. Through His sacrifice on the cross we are declared righteous. Jesus' blood shed on the cross removes the guilt and punishment of our sins. His sacrifice provides salvation. Those who believe and confess Jesus as Lord have the opportunity to be in right relationship (righteousness) and gain a new life in Jesus Christ. *See John 6:37-40, 12:45, 14:16; Colossians 1:16-19; and 1 Timothy 2:5.*

3. **The Function of the Holy Spirit**

    The Holy Spirit is in partnership with the Father and Son to help carry out the mission of the church. He is the one who empowers, teaches, leads, guides, and comforts. He is the power source, the anointing. *See John 16:7, 13 and Acts 1:8.*

It must be understood that though the Father, Son, and Holy Spirit have different functions there is no hierarchy. They operate in the power of agreement. Below are additional scriptural references about the Trinity.

1. **The Father, the Son, and the Holy Spirit are referred to as God.**
   Philippians 1:2; Colossians 2:9; Acts 5:3-5

2. **The Father, the Son, and the Holy Spirit are referred to as Creator.**
   Isaiah 64:8; John 1:3; Colossians 1:15-17; Job 26:13, 33:4

Questions and Answers

1. **Who is the Trinity?**

   _____
   _____
   _____

2. **Provide at least one practical example of the Trinity stated in this chapter. Explain in your own words.**

   _____
   _____
   _____

3. **State the function of the Father, Son, and Holy Spirit.**

   a) Function of the Father:

   _____
   _____
   _____

   b) Function of the Son:

   _____
   _____
   _____

   c) Function of the Holy Spirit:

   _____
   _____
   _____

CHAPTER 5

THE HOLY SPIRIT

THE HOLY SPIRIT

Many denominations, churches, and individuals have different interpretations and understandings about the Holy Spirit. This chapter has some frequently asked questions about the Holy Spirit as well as explanations.

WHO IS THE HOLY SPIRIT?

He is the Spirit of God who lives on the inside of the Christian. The Holy Spirit is not an *it* but a person (Acts 13:2). He is the power source. He is the Comforter, Teacher, Guide, and Helper (John 14:26, 16:13). Every Christian should desire to have the baptism of the Holy Spirit. It is an overflow of God's Spirit (John 7:38). It is like having a Cadillac Escalade fully loaded. The Holy Spirit fully loads the Christian, providing extra benefits and an advantage over the enemy. These extra benefits include the ability to pray God's perfect will (Romans 8:26), to operate in the gifts of the Spirit (chapter 6), and to operate in supernatural power (Mark 16:16-17).

Again, the Holy Spirit is the power source. He is supernatural in existence. Supernatural is anything that occurs beyond natural or human abilities. The power that comes with the Holy Spirit is beyond human ability. This is the same power that endowed Jesus when He worked miracles, signs, and wonders. This supernatural power that enabled Jesus to do signs and wonders was not solely for Jesus. John 14:12 states, *"Most assuredly, I say to you, he who believes in Me, the works that I do he will do also; and greater works than these he will do, because I go to My Father."* In John 16, Jesus speaks of sending the Holy Spirit (Helper) to "guide you into all truth" (v. 13). The Holy Spirit also will empower the Christian to endure, successfully handle, and overcome everyday issues that occur in life. This supernatural power is for every Christian who will receive it. It is the same power Jesus spoke about in Acts 1:8 before ascending into heaven. This is the same power that filled the apostles in the upper room in Acts 2:4. *See Luke 12:12; John 7:39, 14:26, 16:13; Romans 8:14,16; 1 Corinthians 2:10-11; 1 Corinthians 2:13; and Galatians 5:18.*

THE FUNCTION OF THE HOLY SPIRIT

The Holy Spirit is in partnership with God the Father and God the Son to help carry out the mission of the church. He is the one who empowers, teaches, leads, guides, and comforts (Acts 1:8; Luke 12:12; John 14:26, 16:13). The Holy Spirit is the intercessor praying the perfect will of the Father at all times (Romans 8:26). He is the power source, the anointing (Acts 1:8).

BAPTISM OF THE HOLY SPIRIT

The baptism of the Holy Spirit occurs when a Christian receives an overflow of God's Spirit (John 4:13-14, 7:38). The baptism of the Holy Spirit (also referred to as being filled with the Spirit) is evident through speaking in tongues. Tongues are a heavenly language that only God can understand. It is the Spirit of God praying His perfect will. As stated at the beginning of this chapter, every Christian should desire to have the baptism of the Holy Spirit. It is an overflow of God's Spirit (John 7:38). It is like having a luxury car fully loaded. All a Christian has to do is simply ask, and he or she will become filled with His Spirit. The baptism of the Holy Spirit can also be received through the laying on of hands. However, the laying on of hands does not make a person speak in tongues. It is simply a point of contact. Once a Christian has been filled with the Holy Spirit, he or she should ask God for the *gift of tongues* so he or she can speak at any time. Examples of believers being filled with the Holy Spirit are found in the following verses: Acts 8:14-17, 9:17, 10:44, 15:8-9, 19:2-6.

WHAT ARE TONGUES?

Tongues are a heavenly language only God can understand. It cannot be translated, only interpreted as the Holy Spirit reveals. Receiving the baptism of the Holy Spirit will allow a Christian to receive a unique prayer language that can be spoken at any time. This is God praying His perfect will (Romans 8:26). This prayer language can only be understood by God and cannot be translated. However, God can reveal at His discretion what is being prayed through interpretation. Meaning, He will reveal in the native language what is being prayed through the person praying in tongues or another person. Chapter 6 explains the interpretation of tongues in detail. This is extremely powerful because there can be no demonic interference with a Christian's prayers since they cannot be understood. Therefore, it is a guarantee that God's perfect will is being prayed in the heavenly language without hindrance or delay.

WHEN CAN TONGUES (THE HEAVENLY LANGUAGE) BE SPOKEN?

1. **Private Devotional Time (1 Corinthians 14:2, 4)**

   Tongues are direct contact with God and can be used in private devotional time. Praying in tongues will strengthen, empower, comfort, and guide the Christian. It is praying the perfect will of God. Therefore, prayers are rendered according to the perfect will of God. There will be times in which God will reveal what is being prayed and times when He will not. Make certain to be obedient when God gives a prompting to pray in the Holy Spirit.

2. **Corporate Worship and Prayer (1 Corinthians 14:2, 4)**

   Tongues can be spoken in corporate worship services during praise and worship segments.

3. **Tongues Draw the Unbeliever (Acts 2:4, 1 Corinthians 14:20-25)**

   God may use someone to speak in tongues or another foreign language to draw those who do not believe. This is done in a corporate gathering like a worship service. But this can also occur in small group settings. There will always be an interpretation when God uses someone to speak in the heavenly language to address the church or group. An interpretation is necessary so parishioners will understand what has been spoken. Remember, the Holy Spirit operates in an orderly fashion. The Holy Spirit will also use someone to speak a message in a foreign language. This often occurs to spiritually edify those who speak that language. A biblical example would be the Day of Pentecost in Acts 2:5-8. The Holy Spirit was given, and the apostles spoke in other tongues. Those passing heard the gospel preached in their native language.

BENEFITS OF SPEAKING IN TONGUES

1. Spiritual Edification

When you pray in tongues your spirit is praying, and it is in direct contact with God. God is Spirit; therefore, you are talking to Him in a supernatural language (1 Corinthians 14:2).

2. Praying the Perfect Will of God

Praying in tongues guarantees you are praying the perfect will of God (Romans 8:26). Praying in tongues provides a double guarantee; you are praying the perfect will of God, and your prayers cannot be hindered because the devil cannot understand tongues. Remember that tongues can only be interpreted, not translated (1 Corinthians 12:10). You are also praying for the unknown. God will not reveal everything that is prayed in tongues. You have to trust that His perfect will is being done.

3. Stimulates Faith

Jude 20 says, *"But you, beloved, building up your most holy faith, praying in the Holy Spirit."* It takes faith to pray in tongues because you do not know what you are saying. You must trust God's Word that you are praying the perfect will of God (Romans 8:26) though you cannot understand with your human intellect. If you can trust God in this area, it will help you to trust God in other areas of your life. You are strengthening the principle of trusting God, affording you the ability to apply it in any area of your life and any situation.

4. Keeps One Free from Spiritual Contamination

Often times your spirit can be exposed to ungodly things beyond your control. This can be at work, shopping, at the gym, commercials on television, vulgar talk, and so on. We are to be in this world, but not of it. Just as physical things have to be cleaned and maintained, our spirits have to as well. Praying in the Holy Spirit will cleanse our spirits from any and all types of worldly contamination so that seeds of ungodliness will not take root.

Questions and Answers

1. **Who is the Holy Spirit?**

2. **What is the function of the Holy Spirit?**

3. **Explain the baptism of the Holy Spirit in your own words.**

4. **What is the evidence of the baptism of the Holy Spirit?**

5. **What are tongues?**

6. List the three categories in which tongues can be spoken.

   a. _____

   b. _____

   c. _____

7. What are the four benefits of speaking in tongues?

   a. _____

   b. _____

   c. _____

   d. _____

HOW TO RECEIVE THE BAPTISM OF THE HOLY SPIRIT

The baptism of the Holy Spirit can be received in a corporate (church or group) setting or individually. It is important that the individual who is receiving the Holy Spirit is a Christian, has repented of all sin, and does not have unforgiveness toward any individuals. This can block the baptism. It is important to understand that the Holy Spirit has already been given (Acts 2:1-4). It is your responsibility to receive the baptism of the Holy Spirit. Be sure that you are not engaging in sinful behavior or harboring unforgiveness. If so, take a moment and repent of sins and release all unforgiveness. If necessary, review the "Repentance" section in chapter 3.

Use this prayer as a guide:

Prayer to Receive the Baptism of the Holy Spirit

Lord, please forgive me of my sins (name the sin). I repent and take on the mind of Christ concerning this area of my life. I will commit to aligning my actions with the Word of God so that I will not return to sin. I forgive and release everyone who has offended and/or hurt me in any way. I release all the hurt and every offense knowing You bore it on the cross. By every stripe You endured on the cross I am healed and made whole.

1. Pray the following prayer (individual): "Lord, I ask that you baptize me in the Holy Spirit."

   Pray the following prayer (for someone): "Lord, baptize them in the Holy Spirit."

2. You will hear words in your spirit that will not make sense. That is the heavenly language. Do not analyze or try to figure anything out. It will not make sense to your human intellect.

3. Open your mouth and speak by faith. You will begin to speak in tongues. This is the evidence that you have received the Holy Spirit. Let it flow!

4. After you have received the Holy Spirit pray this prayer: "Lord, give me the gift of tongues so I can speak in the heavenly language at any time."

The same method can be followed if you are assisting someone to receive the baptism of the Holy Spirit.

Chapter 6

The Holy Spirit: The Gifts of the Spirit

THE HOLY SPIRIT: THE GIFTS OF THE SPIRIT

This chapter will explain the other benefits of the Holy Spirit. These benefits are referred to as the gifts of the Holy Spirit. These gifts can only be operative to those Christians who have received the baptism or infilling of the Holy Spirit. These gifts enable the Christian to operate beyond human capacity and in the supernatural. There are many examples of Jesus, the apostles, and Christians operating in the gifts of the Spirit. These examples can be found in any of the Gospels (first four books of the New Testament) and the book of Acts. The power and anointing the Holy Spirit provides are available to those Christians who move in faith as the Spirit leads and guides. Any Christian who has been baptized with the Holy Spirit can operate in any of these gifts as the Holy Spirit wills.

The Gifts of the Spirit

The Holy Spirit comes with *gifts* that are purposed to empower the Christian to fulfill the mission of the church, which is winning souls to Christ. The gifts empower the Christian to be victorious in their individual lives and to edify and encourage others. There are nine gifts and they are commonly referred to as "the gifts of the Spirit." *See 1 Corinthians 12:4-11.*

REVELATORY GIFTS

The revelatory gifts reveal facts or strategies. These gifts are also called the prophetic gifts. There are many testimonials of how the revelatory gifts can be used frequently to enhance others and the body of Christ.

1. **Word of Knowledge:** Reveals facts (past or present) about a situation or person that would not ordinarily be known. *See John 4:16-19.*

2. **Word of Wisdom:** Provides instructions or a strategy as to how to handle a particular matter. This gift presents the "what, where, when, who, and how." *See Matthew 17:24-27 and Luke 17:11-14.*

3. **Discerning of Spirits:** This gift allows a person to physically see spirit beings. These spirits can be heavenly beings (angels) or demonic beings (demons). *See Acts 12:5-11, 16:16-18.*

4. **Prophecy:** This gift foretells future events. *See Isaiah 53 and John 12:27-36.*

Note: Any Christian can operate in this form of simple prophecy. Simple prophecy is for edification, exhortation, and comfort to people (1 Corinthians 14:3). Everyone who operates in simple prophecy is not called to the office of a prophet.

MIRACULOUS GIFTS

The miraculous gifts display physical manifestations of the supernatural.

5. **Gift of Faith:** A level of faith that moves into operation when a Christian's individual faith cannot go any further. This is faith that produces miracles. *See John 11:38-44.*

6. **Gift of Healing:** The supernatural manifestation of physical healings. *See Acts 9:36.*

7. **Working of Miracles:** These are occurrences that humans have no control over. They happen supernaturally. *See Luke 9:10-17.*

UTTERANCE GIFTS

The utterance gifts are a form of communication spoken outwardly.

8. **Different Kinds of Tongues:** This gift allows a Christian to speak in a language they do not know. This can be the heavenly language or a foreign language. Refer to chapter 5 for a complete explanation of tongues. *See Acts 2:1-13.*

9. **Interpretation of Tongues:** When God specifically addresses the church, group, or individual in tongues there will always be an interpretation in the native language so the attendees will be able to understand. *See 1 Corinthians 14:6-18.*

Questions and Answers

1. What is the purpose of the gifts of the Spirit?

   _____

   _____

   _____

   _____

2. List the three categories of the gifts of the Spirit.

   a. _____

   b. _____

   c. _____

3. List the individual gifts that belong to each category of the gifts of the Spirit.

   _____

   _____

   _____

   _____

   _____

   _____

CHAPTER 7

Becoming a New Person in Christ

BECOMING A NEW PERSON IN CHRIST

At the moment of salvation, the spirit of a person becomes renewed in Christ. But they may still have areas that need to be conformed to the Word of God. As a teenager, I made a real commitment to the Lord. I gave God a complete and uncompromising YES! But I still had the desire to listen to music that glorified the works of the flesh. Listening to this type of music fed my flesh and birthed desires to do things that were not godly. My newfound commitment produced a hunger to increase my prayer and study time. After consistently reading and praying, I learned I should not have anything to do with unrighteousness (works that glorify the flesh). The music I was listening to was unrighteous. I immediately removed all ungodly music from my music library. As I grew in prayer and study of the Word, the desire to listen to ungodly music was completely gone.

This is the process of becoming a new person in Christ. God will cleanse the spirit so it will be holy and righteous in Him. 2 Corinthians 5:17 says, *"If any man is in Christ he is a new creature. Old things have passed away; behold, all things have become new."* Becoming *new* means you should now live a life that reflects Christ. This chapter will explain the three parts of the human being and the three parts of the soul. This will provide greater insight into how God created humans.

THE HUMAN TRICHOTOMY: SPIRIT, SOUL, BODY

Now may the God of peace Himself sanctify you completely; and may your whole spirit, soul, and body be preserved blameless at the coming of our Lord Jesus Christ.

1 THESSALONIANS 5:23

Human beings have three parts (trichotomy): spirit, soul, and body. This reflects the Trinity (Father, Son, and Holy Spirit). To truly maximize Christianity, the spirit, soul, and body have to experience salvation. Each part has a function it must fulfill in order to maximize Christianity. If your spirit has not experienced regeneration (salvation) it cannot influence your body and soul. It is impossible. All three parts of your humanity have to be in agreement with the Word of God. The Trinity is the perfect example of agreement.

All three functions of the Trinity have to be in agreement to operate in the life of every Christian. What if God did not send Jesus to earth to save us from our sins? What would it benefit a Christian if Jesus never went to the cross? In Luke 22:41-42, Jesus clearly had doubts about dying on the cross. *"And He was withdrawn from them about a stone's throw, and He knelt down and prayed, saying, 'Father, if it is Your will, take this cup away from Me; nevertheless not My will, but Yours, be done.'"* What if the Holy Spirit did not want to come and dwell in the hearts of every Christian, giving them power? We could not maximize our Christianity as God purposed it.

Your spirit immediately experiences salvation when you accept and confess Jesus as Lord. The soul and body now have to go through the process of matching what has happened in your spirit. Therefore, it is imperative that you maintain a connection with God in your personal time and by becoming planted in a local church. All three parts that make up your human existence now have to become new in Christ. Having an understanding of how God created humans will help guide you through the process of becoming new. Even if you have been a Christian for a number of years this will provide assistance to receiving salvation in areas of your life where you have not experienced a complete deliverance.

1. **Spirit:** The real you; your most inner being. This is what gets renewed and rejuvenated by the Spirit of God when you receive salvation (John 3:3).

2. **Soul:** Your soul is made up of three parts: will, intellect, and emotions. This encompasses your decision-making functions, how you think and how you feel (James 1:21; 1 Thessalonians 5:23).

3. **Body:** Your actual physical body. Your body houses your spirit (Genesis 1:26).

THE THREE PARTS OF THE SOUL: WILL, MIND, EMOTIONS

It is important to delve deeper into the soul portion of the human trichotomy. The soul must be submitted to God in order to reflect God. This is the area in which many Christians struggle because there is an unintentional ignorance that this area does not need to experience salvation or that it automatically gets in order at conversion. Many people carry traumatic experiences, childhood occurrences, and past hurts in their souls. Full submission to God in the area of the soul will result in a healthy relationship with God, oneself, and others. This is why it is important to become planted in a local church. This will provide an opportunity to receive individual counseling to obtain deliverance in specific areas.

1. **Will:** This function has to do with your decision-making faculties. If your will is not aligned or in agreement with God's will, you will not fulfill the perfect will of God for your life. Are your desires aligned with the Word of God and God's perfect will for your life? If not, you have some submitting (willful yielding) to do.
   See Psalm 40:8, 143:10; Matthew 12:47-50; Luke 22:42; and John 4:34, 5:30, 6:38.

2. **Mind:** This function of the soul has to do with your thought and decision-making faculties. Are your thinking and decision making founded upon biblical principles? Are your thinking and decision making inspired by the Holy Spirit? It all

revolves around having the mind of Christ. Jesus instructs us in Philippians 2:5 to have the same mind as His (paraphrased). If you are thinking like Jesus you will be like Jesus. Therefore, everything in the Word will manifest itself in your life. Wow! What an overflow and great life to live! *See Psalm 55:18; Proverbs 23:7; Romans 12:2; 1 Corinthians 13:5; Ephesians 4:12; and Philippians 2:5.*

3. **Emotions:** This function of the soul has to do with your feelings. It is important to walk in spiritual maturity and godly wisdom when dealing with your emotions. It is necessary to have your emotions girded and submitted to the Word of God so that your thoughts and behavior remain disciplined and under the control of the Holy Spirit (Ephesians 4:17-19).

THE PHYSICAL BODY

In chapter 1, we read that salvation is for the whole person: spirit, soul, and body. Just as the soul must be submitted to God your physical body must also be submitted to God to reflect salvation and godly behavior. Can the physical body experience salvation and regeneration as the spirit man does? Yes, when it is submitted to the Word of God. Your body will complete actions based upon commands from the brain. When you receive salvation your spirit, soul, and body should be submitted to the Word of God. Submission to the Word of God will produce godly decisions with corresponding physical actions.

> *I appeal to you therefore, brethren, and beg of you in view of [all] the mercies of God, to make a decisive dedication of your bodies [presenting all your members and faculties] as a living sacrifice, holy (devoted, consecrated) and well pleasing to God, which is your reasonable (rational, intelligent) service and spiritual worship.*
>
> *Do not be conformed to this world (this age), [fashioned after and adapted to its external, superficial customs], but be transformed (changed) by the [entire]*

renewal of your mind [by its new ideals and its new attitude], so that you may prove [for yourselves] what is the good and acceptable and perfect will of God, even the thing which is good and acceptable and perfect [in His sight for you].

ROMANS 12:1-2 (AMP)

Questions and Answers

1. List the three parts of the *human trichotomy*.

    a. _____

    b. _____

    c. _____

2. Why is it important for all three parts of the *human trichotomy* to experience salvation?

    _____

    _____

    _____

3. Why is it important for all three parts of the *soul* to experience salvation?

    _____

    _____

    _____

4. List the three parts of the human *soul* and briefly explain their function.

    a. _____

    b. _____

    c. _____

5. Can the physical body experience salvation as the spirit man does?

_____

_____

_____

✓ Self-Check

6. Assess each part of your soul (will, mind, and emotions). List the areas that are not functioning according to the Word of God. The questions listed below will help begin the assessment. But do not allow the starter questions to limit your assessment.

a) Will
- Do I reverence (honor, respect) God?
- Do I obey the Word of God?

_____

_____

_____

b) Mind
- Are my thoughts godly?
- Is my perspective of life, people, and situations viewed from the perspective of the Word of God?

_____

_____

_____

c) Emotions
- Do I harbor unforgiveness?
- Do I treat people with godly love?
- Do I respond with emotional maturity to challenging situations?
- Am I always angry?
- Am I fearful?

_____

_____

_____

NOTES

Chapter 1

1. Sonya Ellerbe, *"Work It Out"* (sermon presentation, United Christian Fellowship Church International, Salisbury, NC, March 15, 2015).

2. *KJV New Testament Greek Lexicon*, s.v. "Anothen," accessed February 13, 2015, http://www.biblestudytools.com/lexicons/greek/nas/anothen.html.

Chapter 3

3. *KJV New Testament Greek Lexicon*, s.v. "Katergazomai," accessed February 13, 2015, http://www.biblestudytools.com/lexicons/greek/kjv/katergazomai.html.

4. *KJV New Testament Greek Lexicon*, s.v. "Christianos," accessed February 13, 2015, http://www.biblestudytools.com/lexicons/greek/kjv/christianos.html.

5. Dennis Clark, interviewed by Sid Roth. Online, *God's Presence 24/7*, http://www.youtube.com, November 5, 2012.

Chapter 4

6. Charlton T. Lewis and Charles Short. *A Latin Dictionary*. Accessed March 19, 2015. http://www.latin-dictionary.net.

PART TWO

Leader Edition
With Teaching Outline

TRANSFORMATION

Maximize Salvation

LEADER EDITION

TRINA NICHELLE MOORE

CONTENTS

How to Use Transformation Leader Edition 1

Chapter 1 *What Is Salvation and Why Is It Necessary?*
    What Is Salvation? 7
    Why Is Salvation Necessary? 9
    Initial Reception of Salvation 20
    Salvation Regenerates 21
    Salvation Is for the *Whole* Person: Spirit, Soul, and Body 23
    The Eternal Result 25
    How to Receive Salvation 26

Chapter 2 *Get Connected, Stay Connected*
    Maintaining Your *God* Connection 32
    Connection 1 – Find the Right Church and Become Planted 32
    Connection 2 – Remain Distraction Free 36
    Connection 3 – Study of God's Word 38
    Connection 4 – Prayer: Dialogue with God 40
    Connection 5 – Fellowship with Other Christians 42
    Suggested Prayer and Study Practices 43
    Necessary Study Tools for All Christians 44

Chapter 3 *Maintaining Salvation*
    Why Must I Maintain A Free Gift? 48
    Christians and Sinners 53
    Repentance 58
    What Is Grace? 63
    Fasting 65
    What If I Still Have Issues After I Become a Christian? 70
    Seven Steps to Maintain Salvation 73

Chapter 4 *The Trinity: Father, Son, and Holy Spirit*
- The Function of the Father 80
- The Function of the Son.. 80
- The Function of the Holy Spirit.. 80

Chapter 5 *The Holy Spirit*
- Who Is the Holy Spirit?... 85
- The Function of the Holy Spirit.. 86
- Baptism of the Holy Spirit 86
- What Are Tongues? 86
- When Can Tongues (the Heavenly Language) Be Spoken? 87
- Benefits of Speaking in Tongues 88
- How to Receive the Baptism of the Holy Spirit 91

Chapter 6 *The Holy Spirit: The Gifts of the Spirit*
- Revelatory Gifts: Word of Knowledge, Word of Wisdom, Discerning of Spirits, Prophecy 96
- Miraculous Gifts: Gift of Faith, Gift of Healing, Working of Miracles 96
- Utterance Gifts: Different Kinds of Tongues, Interpretation of Tongues.......... 97

Chapter 7 *Becoming A New Person in Christ*
- The Human Trichotomy: Spirit, Soul, Body.. 102
- The Three Parts of the Soul: Will, Mind, and Emotions......................... 103
- The Physical Body 104

Notes 109
About the Author.. 111

HOW TO USE TRANSFORMATION LEADER EDITION

The *Transformation Leader Edition* curriculum is written in an outline form, suitable for teaching use for Bible study, small groups, or evangelistic cell groups. This edition includes *Transformation* (individual edition) at the beginning of the book for personal use, and teaching outlines for instructional use. It is **highly** recommended that each teacher or leader completes the individual study prior to presenting to a group. The leader edition includes:

- ✓ All seven chapters outlined for the purpose of teaching
- ✓ Answers for each section highlighted within the outline
- ✓ Responses listed in the Question and Answer sections
- ✓ Group leader suggestions for group activities and discussions

If your church has ministerial staff, leaders, teaching departments, or individuals who need training, the author is available to conduct training sessions. Complete the contact form at www.trinanichellemoore.com.

Questions and Answers

The answers to each question are shaded in gray within the outlines. The numbers that are in parenthesis at the end of a heading or section are page references to *Transformation* (individual edition).

The answers are also provided in the Question and Answer sections. The section in which the answer is located within the teaching outline is in parenthesis after each question, along with the page reference to *Transformation* (individual edition).

Group Discussions

All open-ended assessment questions are located in the Self Check Sections. Follow the Group Leader Suggestions below for guided group discussions. Group discussions are encouraged as it provides accountability and encouragement for those working on their spiritual and practical issues. Church and group leaders should ensure that teaching sessions are safe places for participants to be transparent.

Group Leader Suggestions

1. Provide 5-7 minutes for participants to answer questions individually.

2. For a group of **five or less participants,** provide 1-2 minutes per person to verbally answer each question.

3. For a group of **six or more participants,** divide the class into small groups and have them discuss each question. Provide 2-3 minutes for small group discussion. Bring the group back together and select 2-3 participants to share corporately. Provide 5-7 minutes for corporate sharing.

The Group Leader Suggestions are recommended when the following phrase is stated:

*Refer to the **Group Leader Suggestions** listed in the **How to Use Transformation Leader Edition** section located at the beginning of the curriculum.*

CHAPTER 1

WHAT IS SALVATION *and* WHY IS IT NECESSARY?

I. WHAT IS SALVATION?

A. *Salvation* is deliverance and preservation from sin and its effects, illusion (incorrect perceptions), and destruction (physical/emotional harm, wrong decisions, or anything that is destructive). Salvation also regenerates. To *regenerate* is to remake; restoring to a better state of existence. Therefore, it can be concluded that salvation ***delivers and preserves from sin and its effects, illusion, and destruction, restoring to a better state of existence.*** Salvation is holistic. The spirit, soul (will, mind, emotions), and body can experience salvation. It can make those who have received Jesus Christ *whole*. To be *whole* is ***to be made complete and entire lacking nothing.***

B. Think of an antique piece of furniture that is worn down and not in condition to be used nor seen. This piece of furniture will need to be restored before it is displayed or ready for use. If we allow God (the restorer) into our lives, salvation will remake and restore us to pristine condition (John 10:10). [1]

C. It is very important to understand that salvation cannot be earned through effort or works. Salvation is given to those who confess and believe by faith (Romans 10:9-10). But it does not excuse a Christian from displaying the fruit of their salvation. The fruit, or evidence, of salvation is obedience to the Word of God and the display of godly character (Galatians 5:22-26). The above stated is a direct result of a Christian maintaining their salvation, which is explained in detail in chapter 3.

D. Definition of Salvation: Salvation is ***deliverance*** and ***preservation*** from sin, illusion, and destruction, restoring to a better state of existence.

TRANSFORMATION: LEADER EDITION

Questions and Answers

1. **What is salvation? (Section IA; Page 8)**
   Salvation is _deliverance_ **and** _preservation_ **from** _sin_ **and its effects,** _illusion_ **and** _destruction_ **, restoring to a** _better_ **state of existence.**

2. **What does salvation save you from? (Section IA; Page 8)**
   - Sin and its effects
   - Illusion (incorrect perceptions)
   - Destruction (physical/emotional harm, wrong decisions, or anything that is destructive)

Self-Check

3. **What areas in your life need to experience salvation? In other words, what areas have not experienced regeneration (Page 8)?**

*Refer to the **Group Leader Suggestions** listed in the **How to Use Transformation Leader Edition** section located at the beginning of the curriculum.*

II. WHY IS SALVATION NECESSARY?

A. Adam and Eve (9)

1. God created the first humans, Adam and Eve, to dwell in His presence. He created a beautiful garden, the Garden of Eden, for Adam and Eve to live (Genesis 2:8-25). God gave them free rein of the garden, but they were not to eat from the tree of knowledge of good and evil (Genesis 2:16-17).
   a. The serpent tempted Adam and Eve to disobey God (Genesis 3). This one act of disobedience to God created a legal opening for the results of sin to reign in the earth (Genesis 3:14-19).

2. *Sin* is any action that is contrary to the Word of God.
   a. Obedience and disobedience can manifest two different outcomes.
   b. Godly obedience manifests the blessings (goodness) of God (Deuteronomy 28:1-14).
      1) One of the most important benefits of God's blessings is the privilege and access to have a supernatural connection with God ALL the time.
      2) You can talk to God, and God will talk back to you.
      3) This connection will also provide you with everything needed during each and every season and circumstance that may occur in your life.
      4) Other examples of blessings include (but are not limited to) prosperity, peace, healing, provision, miracles, contentment, and favor.

3. On the other hand, disobedience manifests curses (opposite of blessings).
   a. Examples of curses include (but are not limited to) lack, poverty, sickness, disease, discontentment, strife, contention, and bondage (Deuteronomy 28:15-24).
   b. When Adam and Eve disobeyed God, their actions provided a legal opening for curses to manifest. Genesis 3:14-24 depicts how the curse will manifest. Those manifestations in Genesis 3 included pain in childbearing, hardened soil, death, and eviction from the Garden of Eden.
   c. This curse broke the connection (relationship) between Adam and Eve and God, separating them from His presence.

4. ***Sin*** **and *iniquity* now have legal access in the earth. This is not God's fault, but the result of Adam and Eve's disobedience.**
   a. Humans would have had to endure the consequences of Adam and Eve's sin, which is death on earth and eternity with Satan. Even now, no one is exempt from death, but we have an option with our eternal resting place.
   b. This option is eternal life made possible through Jesus Christ.
   c. You are probably asking the question: How did Jesus provide options to our eternal resting place? Let's go back to Genesis to find the answer.

B. Humans Have Earthly Dominion (10-14)

1. *"Let Us make man in Our image, according to Our likeness; let them have **dominion** over the fish of the sea, over the birds of the air, and over the cattle, over all the earth and over every creeping thing that creeps on the earth." So God created man in His own image; in the image of God He created him; male and female He created them* **(10)**. GENESIS 1:26-27

2. For God to have authority in the earth He must have a human in agreement with His perfect will. God established this in Genesis 1:26-27 when He gave mankind dominion over all the earth (10).
   a. God is the creator of all things. Therefore, He should be able to do anything He desires with complete control, right?
   b. In theory, the answer is yes. In reality, the answer is no. I want to review examples in the Scriptures to prove that God needs a human in agreement to fulfill His will on earth.

3. If My People – 2 Chronicles 7:14-15 (10-11)

In this passage of Scripture, God is responding to Solomon's prayer of dedication (2 Chronicles 6:12-42) for the temple Israel built to worship Him. In 2 Chronicles 7:12, God appeared to Solomon to confirm that He indeed heard his prayer.
   a. Solomon's prayer would be answered if Israel did the following: 1) humble themselves, 2) pray, 3) seek His face, and 4) turn from their wicked ways.

b. If Israel did the aforementioned, God would 1) hear from heaven, 2) forgive their sin, and 3) heal their land (v.14). Obedience releases God to move on our behalf.

c. In 2 Chronicles 7:19-22, God gives a warning to Israel of what would occur if they did not adhere to the instructions in verse 14.

4. No One to Stand in the Gap – Ezekiel 22:29-31 (11)

In this passage of Scripture, God was searching for a qualified leader to move the hearts of the people away from sin.

a. The phrase *make a wall* is metaphoric imagery meaning that God needed a person with enough spiritual influence to turn Israel (God's chosen people) back to God.

b. This leader would need to be one who exemplified a life of godly obedience and could teach the people to do the same.

c. He could not find a suitable leader. As a result (v.31), the people reaped the consequences of sin.

5. Power of Agreement – Matthew 18:19-20; James 4:3 (11-12)

a. This Scripture states that if two individuals agree concerning what they need from the Lord it will be done. Jesus also continues to state that He will be in the midst of those purposely gathered together (in agreement) in His name.

1) It must also be noted that those coming together in agreement must petition God according to His will.

2) 1 John 5:14-15 states, *"Now this is the confidence that we have in Him, that if we ask anything according to His will, He hears us. And if we know that He hears us, whatever we ask, we know that we have the petitions that we have asked of Him."*

b. It is also important to note that the will of God must be spiritually discerned according to individual circumstances and the timing of God.

1) James 4:3 says, *"You ask and do not receive, because you ask **amiss**, that you may spend it on your pleasures."*

2) This Scripture brings out the important fact that prayers should *not* be prayed based upon personal agenda, but according to the perfect will of God for each situation.

c. Let's use a practical example. You are praying for a spouse. There is absolutely nothing wrong with having a desire to marry. God created the institution of marriage. Genesis 2:18 says, *"It is not good that man should be alone; I will make him a helper comparable to him."*
1) You notice an individual of the opposite sex that catches your eye and you begin to pray that that person becomes your spouse. *Stop!*
2) You should first ask God if that person is the spouse He has ordained for you. If God reveals that person is not the spouse He has ordained you are praying **amiss** because that is what you want.
3) You are praying according to the **scriptural** will but not the **perfect** will of God. Though it is correct based upon Scripture, it may not be aligned to the perfect will of God ordained for you.

d. It must be understood that God strategically orders our steps and places people in our paths to fulfill the perfect will of God for our lives. Ultimately, this will further the Kingdom of God. The *perfect will of God* must be known and acted upon.

6. Preach the Gospel – Mark 16:15; Romans 10:14 (12-13)

God is not coming down from heaven to preach the gospel. He commissioned the disciples in Mark 16:15 to do so. Christians, in present times, are disciples (followers of Christ) and are also commissioned to share the gospel.

7. Not Willing that Any Should Perish – 2 Peter 3:9 (13)

This Scripture states that God does not want anyone to perish in his or her sins. He is long-suffering and kind toward us, but He does not excuse sin.

a. Are not people perishing in their sins because they choose not to repent (turn away) from sinful behavior? Yes.
b. If an individual chooses not to follow the way of the Lord they will reap the consequences of their decision.

8. Salvation – Romans 10:9-10 (13)

Salvation is received based upon the individual making the decision to accept. The Scripture states, "That if *you* confess with *your* mouth..." God is not going to force Himself on anyone. Salvation is freely given so that it can be willfully and freely received.

9. Practical Example – Mode of Transportation (13-14)

I want to use a practical example to further explain that God needs a human in agreement to fulfill His will on earth.
a. In our modern society the most common mode of transportation is a car.
b. In order to get from point A to point B, the driver must get in the car, turn it on, and drive to the desired destination.
c. A car cannot travel unless there is someone willing to drive.
d. The will of God is the car. God created humans to do (drive) His will.
e. Christians (driver) are to fulfill God's will; however, He has specific directions (Scriptures) regarding how to get to and from various destinations.
f. Though Christians are the drivers, they are to follow God's directions. God is in control through Christians (humans) in agreement with His will.
g. To sum it up, the will of God is the car, humans are the drivers, God is the GPS!

Questions and Answers

1. **What caused the need for salvation? (Section IIA:1a; Page 14)**

   The serpent tempted Adam and Eve to disobey God (Genesis 3). This one act of disobedience to God created a legal opening for the results of sin to reign in the earth (Genesis 3:14-19).

2. **Genesis 1:26-27 says, "Let Us make man in Our image, according to our likeness; let them have ___dominion___ over the fish of the sea, over the birds of the air, and over the cattle, ___over all the earth___ and over every creeping thing that creeps on the earth. So God created man in His own image; in the image of God He created him; ___male___ and ___female___ He created them. (Section IIB:1; Page 14)**

3. **For God to have ___authority___ in the earth He must have a ___human___ in ___agreement___ with His perfect will. (Section IIB:2; Page 14)**

4. **In 2 Chronicles 7:14-15 what four actions did Israel need to display for their prayers to be answered? (Section IIB:3a; Page 14)**
   - Humble themselves
   - Pray
   - Seek His face
   - Turn from their wicked ways

5. **List at least three Scriptural references from this section that confirm that God needs a human in agreement to fulfill His perfect will. (Section IIB:1-8; Page 15)**
   - If My People – Chronicles 7:14-15
   - No One to Stand in the Gap – Ezekiel 22:29-31
   - Power of Agreement – Matthew 18:19-20; James 4:3

- Preach the Gospel – Mark 16:15; Romans 10:14
- Not Willing that Any Should Perish – 2 Peter 3:9
- Salvation – Romans 10:9-10

Self-Check

6. What has God told you to do (that you have not done) to get in alignment with His word (Page 15)?

*Refer to the **Group Leader Suggestions** listed in the **How to Use Transformation Leader Edition** section located at the beginning of the curriculum.*

C. Jesus, the Unblemished Human

1. Back to the question of origin: How did Jesus provide options to our eternal resting place **(16)**?
   a. Since humans severed the relationship with God through acts of sin, it was necessary for God to have a human to restore it. *(Make reference to the previous section that God gave humans dominion in the earth.)*
   b. God sent His Son, Jesus, to earth as a human through the virgin birth for the ultimate purpose of taking away the sins of the world.
   c. Jesus had to be in agreement with the will of God to die for our sins.

2. *Father, if it is Your will, take this cup away from Me; nevertheless not My will, but Yours, be done. Then an angel appeared to Him from heaven, strengthening Him.*   LUKE 22:42-43

3. God needed an unblemished human to take away the sins of the world. That unblemished human was Jesus Christ **(16)**.
   a. Jesus was born as a human through Mary who was a virgin.
   b. It was a supernatural conception. In other words, no human egg or sperm had anything to do with conceiving Jesus.
   c. The crucifixion of Christ paid the final penalty of sin for the entire human race (Isaiah 53).
   d. Again, the penalty of sin is death on earth and eternity with Satan. Jesus Christ took the penalty in our place. This is how Jesus provided an option to our eternal resting place. Choosing Jesus is choosing eternal life!

4. As noted, God needs a human in agreement with His perfect will **(16)**.
   a. Can you imagine having to sacrifice a loved one for a greater cause? You would most likely try to find an alternative solution.
   b. God knew He gave humans dominion over the earth. Therefore, a human in agreement with His plan of redemption was necessary to restore the relationship between God and mankind through salvation.

c. He demonstrated such integrity that He would not go against His own word even if it meant that His Son, Jesus, would have to die for our sins (Psalm 138:2).
   d. In other words, God did not change the rules in the best interest of His Son.
   e. He honored His word above His own personal interest. He sent His Son to die so those who believe can receive the ultimate benefits of salvation.
   f. Isaiah 53:10 says, *"Yet it pleased the Lord to bruise Him."* Now that is *selfless* love!

5. Jesus' death on the cross symbolizes the end of the reign of sin and its destruction in the life of a Christian **(17)**.
   a. Before Jesus Christ (Old Testament), the priests of God were required to sacrifice an unblemished animal to atone for human sin.
   b. Jesus (the High Priest) was the final unblemished sacrifice for the atonement of sin for all of mankind. His crucifixion paid the final penalty for our sins (Hebrews 9:1-15).

6. The natural act following death is burial. Jesus' burial is symbolic of sin being buried or done away with **(17)**.

7. Finally, Jesus' miraculous resurrection from the grave proves that He is the Savior of the world and He came to give new life abundantly (John 10:10) **(17)**.
   a. The resurrection is symbolic of becoming new in Christ and the new covenant of salvation God has afforded to those who believe (Romans 10:9-10; 2 Corinthians 5:17).
   b. This redemption has restored the relationship between God and mankind as it was with Adam and Eve before sin.
   c. Now a relationship is attainable through receiving the gift of salvation through Jesus Christ.

8. Jesus Christ became us when He took our sins on the cross **(17)**.
   a. Through His redemption, those who receive Him will become new in Him.

Salvation makes us one with Christ.

b. Therefore, we are joint heirs with Him with all of heaven's resources open to us.

c. Jesus Christ prayed this in Matthew 6:10, "*Your kingdom come. Your will be done on earth as it is in heaven.*"

1) *The Spirit Himself bears witness with our spirit that we are children of God, and if children, then heirs—heirs of God and joint heirs with Christ, if indeed we suffer with Him, that we may also be glorified together.*

ROMANS 8:16-17

2) *For there is one God and one Mediator between God and men, the man Christ Jesus, who gave Himself a ransom for all.* 1 TIMOTHY 2:5-6

3) *The thief does not come except to steal, and to kill, and to destroy. I have come that they may have life, and that they may have it more abundantly.* JOHN 10:10

4) *Therefore, if anyone is in Christ, he is a new creation; old things have passed away; behold, all things have become new.* 2 CORINTHIANS 5:17

9. It is important to understand that Jesus was truly human in spirit, soul, and body **(18)**.

   a. He did not have any special privileges or powers when He came to earth because He was the Son of God.

   b. He was stripped of his godly deity. Hebrews 4:15 says, "*[He] was in all points tempted as we are, yet without sin.*"

   c. While on earth Jesus had the potential to sin, was tempted by sin, but did not sin.

   d. Not only was it Jesus' purpose to come to earth and take away the sins of the world, but He was the ultimate example of how to live a victorious life without sin.

   e. He was able to do so because He loved His Father (God) above anything else.

10. Love is a choice with the appropriate actions displayed **(18)**.

    a. John 14:15 says, "*If you love Me, keep My commandments.*"

b. God is love (1 John 4:8).

c. In the beginning was the Word, and the Word was God (John 1:1).

d. God is love, and God is the Word.

e. Therefore, to love God means to keep His commandments, for His commandments are His written Word. In simple terms, *DO* the Word.

　1) If the Word says repent, then you do it. If it says love your neighbor, then do it. If it says pray and study the Scriptures, then be obedient and do it. I believe you get the point!

11. Second, Jesus knew sinful behavior would not please His Father, nor was it in the commandments (Word of God) **(18)**.

a. He knew it was absolutely necessary to maintain a consistent connection with His Father so He would be strong enough to resist sin.

b. This connection is what gave Him the power He needed to be obedient and to stay focused on fulfilling His assignment (death, burial, and resurrection).

Questions and Answers

1. **Why was it necessary for Jesus to come to earth as a human? (Section IIC:1a-c; Page 19)**
   - Since humans severed the relationship with God through acts of sin, it was necessary for God to have a human to restore it.
   - God sent His Son, Jesus, to earth as a human through the virgin birth for the ultimate purpose of taking away the sins of the world.
   - Jesus had to be in agreement with the will of God to die for our sins.
   - **Summation of Answer:** God needed an unblemished human that would die for our sins.

2. **What do the death (crucifixion), burial, and resurrection symbolize (Page 19)?**
   - **Death (crucifixion):** Jesus' death on the cross symbolizes the end of the reign of sin and its destruction in the life of a Christian. **(Section IIC:5)**
   - **Burial:** The natural act following death is burial. Jesus' burial is symbolic of sin being buried or done away with. **(Section IIC:6)**
   - **Resurrection:** The resurrection is symbolic of becoming new in Christ and the new covenant of salvation God has afforded to those who believe (Romans 10:9-10; 2 Corinthians 5:17). This redemption has restored the relationship between God and mankind as it was with Adam and Eve before sin. **(Section IIC:7a-b)**

3. **Did Jesus have any special privileges as the Son of God while He was on earth?**
   (Section IIC:9a-b; Page 19)
   It is important to understand that Jesus was truly human in spirit, soul, and body. He did not have any special privileges or powers when He came to earth because He was the Son of God. He was stripped of his godly deity. Hebrews 4:15 says, *"[He] was in all points tempted as we are, yet without sin."*

4. **How was Jesus able to live a victorious life without sin (Page 19)?**
   - He was the ultimate example of how to live a victorious life without sin. He was able to do so because He loved His Father (God) above anything else. **(Section IIC:9d-e)**
   - Love is a choice with the appropriate actions displayed. **(Section IIC:10a)**
   - He knew it was absolutely necessary to maintain a consistent connection with His Father so He would be strong enough to resist sin. This connection is what gave Him the power He needed to be obedient and to stay focused on fulfilling His assignment (death, burial, and resurrection). **(Section IIC:11a-b)**

   Summation of Answer: Jesus loved God. Jesus displayed His love through obedience to His commandments. Jesus knew that it was necessary to maintain a relationship with God to maintain the power needed to live free from sin.

5. **John 14:15 states, "If you love Me, keep My commandments." (Section IIC:10a; Page 19)**

*Refer to the **Group Leader Suggestions** listed in the **How to Use Transformation Leader Edition** section located at the beginning of the curriculum.*

III. INITIAL RECEPTION OF SALVATION

A. *"That if you confess with your mouth the Lord Jesus and believe in your heart that God has raised Him from the dead, you will be saved. For with the heart one believes unto righteousness, and with the mouth confession is made unto salvation."* ROMANS 10:9-10

1. This passage of Scripture explains how to receive salvation. One must *confess* and believe in Jesus Christ and **make Him Lord** in his or her life.
2. When one confesses Jesus as Lord, He becomes the final authority in a Christian's life.
3. This means there is complete obedience to the Word of God. For a more in-depth review, read the passage of Scripture below taken from the Amplified Bible:
    a. "Because if you acknowledge and confess with your lips that Jesus is Lord and in your heart (inner most being) believe (adheres to, trust in, and rely on truth) that God raised him from the dead, you will be **delivered, liberated and preserved**. For with the heart (inner most being) a person believes (adheres to, trust in, and rely on truth) and so is justified (declared righteous, acceptable to God), and with the mouth he confesses (declares openly and speaks out freely his faith) and confirms [his] **deliverance, liberation, and preservation**." ROMANS 10:9-10 AMP EMPHASIS ADDED

Question and Answer

1. **How does a person receive salvation? (Section IIIA:1; Page 20)**
   - Confess Jesus Christ
   - Believe Jesus Christ
   - Make Jesus Lord

IV. SALVATION REGENERATES

A. I want to review another Scripture passage that speaks of salvation. As stated in the beginning of this chapter, another word or synonym for salvation is *regenerate.*
   1. To *regenerate* is to *remake: restoring to a better state of existence.*
   2. In John 3, Jesus explains salvation to a Pharisee, Nicodemus, using the terminology *born again*.
   3. In John 3:16, Jesus speaks of believing in Him and the work of the cross before it even happened. *"For God so loved the world that He gave His only begotten Son, that whoever believes in Him should not perish but have everlasting life."*
   4. Jesus knew His purpose! The definition of *born again* is explained below in greater detail.

B. *Jesus answered, "Most assuredly, I say to you, unless one is born of water and the Spirit, he cannot enter the kingdom of God. That which is born of the flesh is flesh, and that which is born of the Spirit is spirit. Do not marvel that I said to you, **'You must be born again.'** The wind blows where it wishes, and you hear the sound of it, but cannot tell where it comes from and where it goes. So is everyone who is born of the Spirit."*   JOHN 3:5-8

C. Details of *Born Again*
   1. **Born:** To bring forth or brought forth
   2. **Again (*Anothen* in Greek):** From above, from a higher place; anew, over again[2]
   3. **Regenerate:** To remake; restoring to a better state of existence

D. Born Again - Definition
   1. **Born Again:** Brought forth anew to a better state of existence

E. Now, read John 3:5-8 (NKJV) with the definition of "born again" as stated above: *Most assuredly, I say to you, unless one is **brought forth anew** of water and the Spirit, he cannot enter the kingdom of God. That which is **brought forth** of the flesh is flesh, and that which is **brought forth** of the Spirit is spirit. Do not marvel that I said to you, 'You must* be ***brought forth anew.****' The wind blows where it wishes, and you hear the sound of it, but cannot tell where it comes from and where it goes. So is everyone who is **brought forth** of the Spirit.*

F. Another Scripture verse that supports the newness that accompanies salvation is 2 Corinthians 5:17, *"Therefore, if any man be in Christ he is a new creation; old things have passed away; behold, all things have become new."*

Question and Answer

1. **What does it mean to be *born again*? (Section IVD; Page 22)**

    To be brought forth anew to a better, higher, or more worthy state of existence.

V. SALVATION IS FOR THE WHOLE PERSON: SPIRIT, SOUL, AND BODY

A. A Christian receives salvation when he or she confesses and believes in Jesus Christ (Romans 10:9-10). *A Christian can also experience salvation beyond the point of praying the prayer of salvation.*
   1. Salvation is everlasting (perpetual, enduring) in nature.
      a. It first occurs spiritually (by receiving Jesus as Lord; salvation) and should bear fruit in the natural (behavior).
      b. The saving power of Jesus can and should be a perpetual experience in the life of a Christian.
      c. This can only happen when a Christian is **consistently connected** and **obedient** to the Word of God.
      d. Hebrews 4:12 proves that God (John 1:1) desires that His saving grace make us clean and whole in every area.

B. *"For the Word that God speaks is alive and full of power [making it active, operative, energizing, and effective]; it is sharper than any two-edged sword, penetrating to the dividing line of the breath of life (soul) and [the immortal] spirit, and of joints and marrow [of the deepest parts of our nature], exposing and sifting and analyzing and judging the very thoughts and purposes of the heart."* HEBREWS 4:12 AMP

C. The definition of salvation stated at the beginning of this chapter, and in Hebrews 4:12, establishes that salvation is for all parts that make up the human being: spirit, soul (will, mind, emotions), and body. Therefore, the effects of salvation make the person who receives **whole**.
   1. To be whole is ***to be made entire and complete, lacking nothing.***

D. The word ***made*** indicates there is a process to becoming whole.
   1. When something is made, a process must be followed before the finished product can be presented.

2. The results are not always instant. Be willing to take the time to experience salvation in those areas of difficulty.

E. Galatians 6:9 states, *"And let us not grow weary while doing good, for in due season we shall reap if we do not lose heart."*
   1. **Due season** does not have a time limit because it can be different for each individual.
   2. James 1:4 says, *"But let patience have its perfect work, that you may be perfect and complete, lacking nothing."*
      a. The Lord knows what it is going to take for each of His children to be complete and lacking nothing.
      b. Do not be afraid to exercise patience. Salvation is not magic.
      c. Be willing to yield to the salvation process and see the results manifested in your life.

Questions and Answers

1. **How can a Christian experience the perpetual (enduring) benefits of salvation? (Section VA:1b-c; Page 24)**

    The saving power of Jesus can and should be a perpetual experience in the life of a Christian. This can only happen when a Christian is *consistently connected* and *obedient* to the Word of God.

2. **What makes up the *whole person*? (Section VC; Page 24)**

    The human being: spirit, soul (will, mind, emotions), and body.

3. **What does it mean to be made *whole*? (Section VC:1; Page 24)**

    To be whole is to be made entire and complete, lacking nothing.

4. **The word __made__ indicates there is a __process__ to becoming whole. (Section VD; Page 24)**

5. **Galatians 6:9 says:** "And let us not grow weary while doing good, for in due season we shall reap if we do not lose heart." **(Section VE; Page 24)**

6. **__Due season__ does not have a time limit because it can be different for each individual. (Section VE:1; Page 24)**

7. **James 1:4 says,** "But let patience have its perfect work, that you may be perfect and complete, lacking nothing." **(Section VE:2; Page 24)**

*Refer to the **Group Leader Suggestions** listed in the **How to Use Transformation Leader Edition** section located at the beginning of the curriculum.*

VI. THE ETERNAL RESULT

A. There is an eternal result of salvation. It is the inheritance of eternal life with God once this earthly life is over. Those who are unsaved will spend eternity in hell with Satan.

1. Heaven

Heaven is the place where God, Jesus, and the Holy Spirit live. All Christians who believe in Jesus Christ and fulfill His will are rewarded with eternal life in heaven. *See Revelation 22:14; Matthew 25:46; John 3:3-7, 4:14, 5:24, 8:51, 11:25-26.*

2. Hell

Those who do not believe, do not accept Jesus as Lord nor obey His commands will be sent to hell to suffer for eternity. *See Matthew 25:41-43; 2 Peter 2:3-9; Revelation 19:20; Mark 16:16; Romans 13:2; 1 Corinthians 6:8-10; Galatians 5:19-21; 1 Timothy 5:12.*

VII. HOW TO RECEIVE SALVATION

A. If you are reading this book and have not accepted the Lord Jesus Christ as your personal Savior, please read the "Steps to Receive Salvation" section below and pray the prayer of salvation. If you were once saved and have turned away from God, you also can pray the prayer of salvation and recommit your life to the Lord. Remember that it is not your actions that produce salvation. It is believing, confessing, and receiving Jesus as Lord (sole authority) in your life.

B. Steps to Receive Salvation
1. **Admit** that you have sinned, confess (to God) your sins and repent (turn away from sin).*
2. **Believe** in your heart (innermost being, spirit, the real you) that Jesus Christ died for your sins and God raised Him from the dead.
3. **Confess** (speak aloud) that Jesus Christ is Lord in your life.
4. Immediately begin attending a Bible-based, Holy Spirit-filled church.

C. Prayer of Salvation

Lord Jesus Christ, I am sorry for the things I have done wrong in my life. I ask your forgiveness and now turn (repent) from everything I know is wrong according to the Word of God. I believe You died on the cross to set me free from my sins and were resurrected so that I can have a new life in You. Please come into my life and fill me with Your Holy Spirit. Amen.

D. Get Connected

Praise God! If you have prayed the prayer of salvation make it a priority to **immediately** get connected with other strong Christians and begin attending a Spirit-filled church that teaches the Word of God in truth. Read more about getting connected in the next chapter. Chapter 3 "Maintaining Salvation" will take you through the steps of applying salvation into every area of your life.

*Refer to the section on Repentance in chapter 3 for an in depth explanation.

CHAPTER 2

GET CONNECTED, STAY CONNECTED

Once a commitment is made to Christianity, it is vitally important to stay connected to God. Many individuals commit their lives to the Lord without immediately connecting with a church and other strong Christians. As a result, they find themselves spiritually weak and uncommitted to the Lord. Hebrews 10:24-25 says, *"And let us consider one another in order to stir up love and good works, not forsaking the assembling of ourselves together, as is the manner of some, but exhorting one another, and so much the more as you see the Day approaching."*

This chapter will present five connection steps to maintain a connection with God. This can be compared to taking prescription medication for an illness. Medication is prescribed to treat the ailment so it does not grow worse. The ailment of a non-Christian is living a life apart from God, the Creator. Maintaining your connection with God will keep you spiritually strong.

Maintaining Your God Connection

I. CONNECTION 1
FIND THE RIGHT CHURCH AND BECOME PLANTED
PSALM 92:12-14; EPHESIANS 4:11-16

A. *The righteous shall flourish like a palm tree, He shall grow like a cedar in Lebanon. Those who are planted in the house of the* Lord *shall flourish in the courts of our God. They shall still bear fruit in old age; they shall be fresh and flourishing…"* PSALM 92:12-14

B. Often times, individuals choose a church based upon their preferences and levels of comfort **(32)**.
   1. A church should be chosen through the leading of the Holy Spirit.
   2. The church in which you become planted will be a place to serve as well as to be

equipped to fulfill your God-ordained purpose.

3. Such a church will uphold the standards of the Bible. If not, run!

C. *"And He Himself gave some to be apostles, some prophets, some evangelists, and some pastors, and teachers, for the **equipping** of the saints… till we all come to the unity of the faith and of the knowledge of the Son of God, to a perfect (mature) man (mankind), to the measure of the stature of the fullness of Christ."* EPHESIANS 4:12-13

1. The purpose of the church is to equip Christians to become spiritually mature to bring others to Christ and fulfill their God-ordained purpose **(32)**.
    a. To be equipped is to have everything needed to achieve an intended goal or result.
    b. The ministry gifts (apostle, prophet, evangelist, pastor, and teacher) are for the equipping of the saints.
    c. These individuals are responsible for providing the saints (Christians) what is needed (teaching of the Word, correction, and advisement) to live victoriously in Christ.

2. Verse 13 gives the result of being equipped. Being equipped will cause the saints to be **(32)**:
    a. (1) Unified in the faith (in Christ)
    b. (2) Knowledgeable of the Son of God (Christ)
    c. (3) A perfect (mature) Christian
    d. (4) To experience the fullness and completeness that comes with knowing Christ

    *The numbers used to identify the answers above are used in Transformation Original Edition. The leader can refer to the numbers when reviewing this section with participants.

D. As a Christian it is your responsibility to become planted in the church God has chosen **(33)**.

1. Becoming planted can take on many different functions. For example, this

includes working in a ministry area that best suits your gifts and abilities, leadership roles and much more.

2. For the sake of this writing, only the foundational aspect of being planted will be addressed. ***The foundational action of becoming planted is to join a church and maintain consistent attendance at regularly scheduled services so that your spirit will receive spiritual nourishment from the Word of God.*** This is non-negotiable.

E. When an object is planted, it is stationary in one place getting the necessary nourishment to remain vital, healthy and strong **(33)**.
  1. Psalm 1:3 says, *"He shall be like a tree* **planted** *by the rivers of water, that brings forth fruit in its season, whose leaf also shall not wither; and whatever he does shall prosper."*
  2. Becoming planted in a local church results in a vital, healthy, and strong relationship with Christ.

Questions and Answers

1. **What is the purpose of the church? (Section IC:1; Page 33)**

   The purpose of the church is to equip Christians to become spiritually mature to bring others to Christ and fulfill their God-ordained purpose.

2. **What does it mean to be *planted* in a church? (Section ID:2; Page 33)**

   The foundational action of becoming planted is to join a church and maintain consistent attendance at regularly scheduled services so that your spirit will receive consistent spiritual nourishment from the Word of God.

3. **What are the results of becoming *planted*? (IE:2; Page 33)**

   Becoming planted in a local church results in a vital, healthy, and strong relationship with Christ.

*Refer to the **Group Leader Suggestions** listed in the **How to Use Transformation Leader Edition** section located at the beginning of the curriculum.*

How Do I Know When God Is Leading Me to Become Planted In A Church?

God desires that every Christian become planted in a local church. If you have not found a church or do not attend consistently, make a commitment to seek God regarding where you should become planted. The following are some questions to help determine where God desires for you to be planted. Place a "Y" for yes or "N" for no next to each question below **(34)**.

1. Does the pastor or designee preach and teach messages that are in proper alignment with the Bible providing scriptural references so that you can study in your personal time? _____

2. Is there peace in your spirit when you attend? Is there peace in your spirit even if the sermon deals with personal situations that may be uncomfortable? _____

3. Do you receive specific strategies and solutions to personal situations in your life during the services? (This can include sermons, Sunday school/Bible study lessons, and prophetic sayings.) _____

4. Have you experienced positive results by acting upon the teachings and strategies taught during services? _____

5. Are you spiritually challenged to go beyond your present spiritual level? _____

If your answer is yes to all of the above stated questions, it is a good indication that God may be leading you to become planted in this specific church. You may need to consider other factors along with these questions. Remain prayerful and seek wise, godly counsel. God will always reveal and confirm His perfect will for you.

Self-Check

1. Based upon the questions in the previous survey, assess where you are currently attending church. Have you chosen this church based upon your personal preferences and opinions, or where God is leading you? **(Page 35)**

2. Are you planted? What evidence do you see to prove your answer? **(Page 35)**

*Refer to the **Group Leader Suggestions** listed in the **How to Use Transformation Leader Edition** section located at the beginning of the curriculum.*

II. CONNECTION 2
REMAIN "DISTRACTION" FREE

A. *Be sober, be vigilant; because your adversary the devil walks about like a roaring lion, seeking whom he may devour. Resist him, steadfast in the faith, knowing that the same sufferings are experienced by your brotherhood in the world.* 1 PETER 5:8-9

B. Many Christians allow distractions to pull them away from staying connected to the activities and people God has divinely appointed to help them in their Christian walk. These distractions can be jobs, friends, family, or even relationships. If people or things pose a distraction to your spiritual connection, remove them immediately.

 Self-Check

1. List people, relationships or things that are a distraction to your Christian faith (Page 37).

2. What steps will you take to remove the distractions listed above (Page 37)?

3. List any distractions that may be difficult for you to remove on your own. Make a commitment to share with another mature Christian. This will provide support, instruction and accountability to remove these distractions (Page 37).

Refer to the **Group Leader Suggestions** *listed in the* **How to Use Transformation Leader Edition** *section located at the beginning of the curriculum.*

III. CONNECTION 3
STUDY OF GOD'S WORD

A. A Christian should develop a consistent habit of reading and studying God's Word in addition to communing with God in prayer.

1. **Study God's Word**

    Psalm 119:105; John 1:1-5; Matthew 4:4; John 6:32-35; 1 Corinthians 10:3-4

    a. *Be diligent to present yourself approved to God, a worker who does not need to be ashamed, rightly dividing the word of truth.* 2 TIMOTHY 2:15

    b. **Private Bible study:** Private Bible study should *always* include the teachings and sermons taught at Sunday school or small group, Sunday worship service, and mid-week services. This includes *finding, confessing, and meditating* on Scripture that deal with a specific area to be improved. For example, if there is an issue with speaking negative about oneself or situations, a verse should be found that provides a resolve against negative talking. Ephesians 4:29 says, *"Let no corrupt word proceed out of your mouth, but what is good for necessary edification, that it may impart grace to the hearers."* This is where a topical Bible, such as *Be Like Jesus Scriptures for Transformation*, will be very useful. It has the Scriptures listed by topics and categories, and it is a good companion to this curriculum.

    c. **Confessing God's Word:** The Bible says, *"You shall have what you say"* (paraphrase of Mark 11:23). Therefore, if certain situations are not reflecting the Word (Scripture), then you need to speak the Word until you see those situations change. Speaking the Word will also strengthen your faith to believe God for what is needed. *See Psalm 119:172; Proverbs 10:11; Mark 11:22-24; and Hebrews 4:14, 10:23.*

    d. **Meditating on God's Word:** To meditate means to "mutter over and over; engage in thought or contemplation; reflect." Joshua 1:8 says, *"This Book of the Law shall not depart from your mouth, but you shall meditate in it day and night, that you may observe to do according to all that is written in it. Then you will make your way prosperous and then you will have good success."* Meditating is taking the time to focus solely on God's Word through thought and speech, getting it deep into the spirit. *See Psalm 77:12, 104:34, 119:23, 143:5; and 1 Timothy 4:13,15.*

Self-Check

1. **Assess your study time on a scale of 1-4 for the categories below (Page 39).**
   (**1** – I do not engage; **2** – I engage 1-2 times/week; **3** – I engage 3-4 times/week; **4** – I engage 5 times or more/week)

   - **Private Bible study:**
   - **Confessing God's Word:**
   - **Meditating on God's Word:**

2. For the areas receiving a score of a 1 or 2, develop and write out weekly goals to achieve a level 3 or 4 engagement score. Use the space below to develop and write your goals. Refer to the "Suggested Prayer and Study Practices," at the end of this chapter for suggestions of how to begin (Page 39).

*Refer to the **Group Leader Suggestions** listed in the **How to Use Transformation Leader Edition** section located at the beginning of the curriculum.*

IV. CONNECTION 4
PRAYER: DIALOGUE WITH GOD

PSALM 5:3, 40:1; JEREMIAH 23:23; MATTHEW 18:19-20; HEBREWS 4:16; 1 JOHN 5:14-15

A. Two-Way Conversation: Prayer does not only consist of the Christian talking to God. God also wants to talk to you. Do not get locked into a one-way conversation.

B. Learning God's Voice: In general, God will speak through the conscience (thoughts), which is the voice of the human spirit.
  1. Have you ever had a thought that something just was not right or that you should do something at a particular time? That is God speaking through your human spirit.
  2. By feeding your spirit the Word of God, it will be trained to hear the voice of God.
  3. John 10:4 states, *"And the sheep follow him, for they know his voice."*
      a. In this passage, Christians are referred to as sheep.
      b. Sheep follow the shepherd, which is God.
      c. Learning to recognize God's voice is powerful. He will begin to speak in a more detailed and intimate manner.
      d. Keeping a pure mind and spirit, maintaining a godly atmosphere, and consistency in the Word and prayer guarantee open dialogue with God.

Self-Check

1. How often do you pray? Assess your prayer time on a scale of 1-4 (Page 41).
   (**1** – I do not engage; **2** – I engage 1-2 times/week; **3** – I engage 3-4 times/week; **4** – I engage 5 times or more/week)

2. If your engagement score is a 1 or 2, develop and write out weekly goals to achieve a level 3 or 4 engagement score. Use the space below to develop and write your goals. Refer to the "Suggested Prayer and Study Practices," at the end of this chapter for suggestions of how to begin (Page 41).

*Refer to the **Group Leader Suggestions** listed in the **How to Use Transformation Leader Edition** section located at the beginning of the curriculum.*

TRANSFORMATION: LEADER EDITION

V. CONNECTION 5
FELLOWSHIP WITH OTHER CHRISTIANS
ACTS 2:42-43, 46-47; HEBREWS 10:24-25

A. *And let us consider one another in order to stir up love and good works, not forsaking the assembling of ourselves together, as is the manner of some, but exhorting one another, and so much the more as you see the Day approaching.*   HEBREWS 10:24-25

B. The Bible clearly states that Christians are to fellowship with other Christians to remain encouraged and strengthened.
  1. This was evident in the early church in the book of Acts (Acts 2:42).
  2. They were always fellowshipping and strengthening themselves in their new-found faith.
      a. Christianity was a new faith, and often times Christians were persecuted simply for believing in Christ.
      b. They consistently strengthened and encouraged one another so that the possibility of persecution would not cause them to turn from Christ.

C. Make it a priority to attend church-sponsored fellowships, outings, and church services. This will provide opportunities to be around other strong Christians.

Self-Check

---

1. Evaluate the company you keep. Do these individuals encourage you to maintain your relationship with the Lord and obedience to His word **(Page 42)**?

   *Refer to the **Group Leader Suggestions** listed in the **How to Use Transformation Leader Edition** section located at the beginning of the curriculum.*

VI. SUGGESTED PRAYER AND STUDY PRACTICES

Every Christian needs to have uninterrupted time with God. Below is a suggested outline of how to develop a habit of one-on-one time with God.

A. First Fruits – Beginning the Day
   1. **Praise and Thanksgiving - 15 minutes**
      a. This is time when you simply thank God for who He is and for the blessings He has bestowed upon your life. You can include Scripture verses of praise. The book of Psalms is a great place to start. You can also praise God in the Holy Spirit (tongues). Refer to chapter 5 "The Holy Spirit" for an in-depth explanation.

   2. **Reading and Meditating on Scripture - 15 minutes**
      a. God may lay a particular Scripture on your heart, or you can refer to verses on a specific area you are dealing with. You can also refer to verses from the sermon at previous services.

   3. **Proclamations to "Speak Over Your Day" – 1-2 Minutes**
      a. Take a few moments to command your day. You tell the day what it is going to be.
      Examples include, but are not limited to:
      This day will be successful and productive.
      I will walk in the favor of God.
      I will progress and prosper in all things today.
      My body is healed, and I am strong.
      b. Scriptural proclamations:
      I am the head and not the tail (Deuteronomy 28:13).
      No weapon formed against me shall prosper (Isaiah 54:17).
      I can do all things through Christ that strengthens me (Philippians 4:13).
      My God shall supply all of my needs according to His riches in glory (Philippians 4:20).

VII. NECESSARY STUDY TOOLS FOR ALL CHRISTIANS

A. Study Bible
1. Obtain a study Bible in a version you can understand. The New King James Version, The Amplified Bible, and The New Living Translation Bible are versions that are easy to understand.
2. A study Bible will have a commentary section that will explain the proper interpretations of the Scripture passages you are reading.

B. Topical Bible or Bible Promise Book
1. This is a Bible that is organized by topic. For example, if the issue is anger, it will list verses on that topic. The title may be Topical Bible or Promise Book; however, they serve the same purpose. *Be Like Jesus Scriptures for Transformation* is highly recommended.

C. Concordance
1. A concordance lists Scripture based upon key words.
2. The verse, "I can do all things through Christ that gives me strength," can be found by looking up ***strength***.
3. It will list the book and verse where it can be found in the Bible.
4. There will also be other verses that include the word ***strength***. If Scripture verses for a particular word or topic are needed, the concordance will list all the verses accordingly. For example, if verses for ***salvation*** are needed, the concordance will list all those that have the word ***salvation*** in them.

D. A local or online Christian bookstore retailer can assist with locating these items.

CHAPTER 3

Maintaining Salvation

Hallelujah! You have taken the initial step of receiving salvation by believing, confessing, and making Jesus Christ Lord. From this point forward, it is vital that you maintain your free gift of salvation.

I. WHY MUST I MAINTAIN A FREE GIFT?

A. Christianity is a lifestyle rooted in love through a relationship with Jesus Christ **(48)**.

   1. As noted in chapter 1, salvation is everlasting (perpetual, enduring) in nature. It is a continual process in the life of a Christian beyond initial conversion.
   2. The perpetual nature of salvation is manifested through a relationship with Christ.
      a. Love is what caused Jesus to go to the cross to bear our sins.
      b. Love always gives back.
      c. It should not be burdensome to live according to God's commandments (John 14:15; 1 John 5:3).
      d. A Christian lifestyle requires one to develop a mentality and perspective that is based from the Word of God and cultivated through the spirit of God (Philippians 2:5).
      e. John 15:4 states, *"Abide in Me, and I in you. As the branch cannot bear fruit of itself, unless it abides in the vine, neither can you, unless you abide in Me."*

B. To maintain something is to keep in existence preserving from decline **(48)**.

   1. To maintain something, it first must be received.
      a. When you received Jesus Christ as your personal Savior, you received salvation.
   2. Again, salvation is ***deliverance*** and ***preservation*** from sin, illusion, and destruction, restoring to a better state of existence.
   3. Salvation is a free gift. It cannot be earned, nor obtained through works.

4. If salvation is to remain in perpetual existence as God intended, the Christian lifestyle (relationship with God) must be maintained through prayer, study, attending church, and other activities as stated in the "Seven Steps to Maintaining Salvation" section located at the end of this chapter.

C. Receiving Salvation (48)

1. One believes and confesses Jesus Christ.

2. Jesus Christ is Lord (sole authority) in a Christian's life.

3. Salvation is freely given and does not have to be earned.

D. Maintaining Salvation (49)

Nurturing the gift of salvation so that the gift remains in perpetual (continuous) existence through:

1. Getting planted in a local church

2. Prayer and Bible study

3. Maintaining a godly atmosphere

E. Practical Example of Maintaining Salvation (49)

1. If someone were to give me a car, I would be ecstatic! This would mean no debt! Though the car was given to me free and clear, it does not dismiss the reality that I will need to maintain the servicing of the car.

   a. First, I need to keep gas in the car so that I can get to my destinations.

   b. Second, a car needs oil and fluid changes, tire rotations and balances, and additional services required to maintain performance.

      1) If I do not maintain the service requirements for my free car it will not perform at its maximum potential.

      2) Its life span will decline quickly, ultimately resulting in loss.

   c. Salvation is the car without debt.

   d. The giver of the car is Jesus Christ.

   e. A relationship with Jesus Christ is the gas. It keeps everything moving.

MAINTAINING SALVATION

    f. The servicing of the car is consistent prayer, study of God's Word, and getting planted in a local church.

2. If I want my car to perform at its best
   a. I am going to make sure I acquire the best maintenance. I am going to fill up the car with a high quality grade of gas to ensure maximum performance.
      1) My relationship with God is high grade.
      2) I intentionally make time for God both privately and corporately (church).
      3) I may have to get up a bit earlier to give Him the first part of my day.
      4) I guard my time with the Lord by eliminating all distractions.
   b. When it is time for my car to be serviced, I do not procrastinate, nor become neglectful.
      1) When I take my car to be serviced I want honest and skillful mechanics that are knowledgeable of my particular vehicle and can provide the service and proper recommendations.
   c. I maintain my spiritual servicing by attending church each week and engaging in personal Bible study and prayer **(50)**.
      1) My pastor (mechanic) knows my spiritual needs because it is the church where God has planted me.
      2) I am exposed to truth and fresh spiritual perspectives from God that provides new and deeper insight into the Scriptures.
      3) I also receive confirmation in regards to what God has shared with me in my personal time.

3. My intentional efforts to give God my best and to get the best spiritual nourishment move me from a state of religion to relationship.

4. Therefore, Christianity becomes a lifestyle geared towards an intimate relationship with Jesus Christ.

F. Work It Out (50)

1. I want to provide a scriptural reference for the practical example from Philippians 2:12-13:

    a. *Work out your own salvation with fear and trembling; for it is God who works in you both to will and to do for His good pleasure* (New King James Version).

    b. *Work hard to show the results of your salvation, obeying God with deep reverence and fear. For God is working in you, giving you the desire and the power to do what pleases him* (New Living Translation).

2. Two different translations were used because I want to bring clarity to what the Apostle Paul was implying with the word **work**.

    a. The phrase **work out** as stated in the New King James Version originates from the Greek word *Katergazomai* meaning "to do that from which something results of things: bring about, result in."[3]

    b. The word **work** in the context of this Scripture does not indicate that salvation is obtained through merited works.

    c. **Work** is used in the context of intentional effort.

      1) An intentional effort to nurture and maintain your gift of salvation brings about or results in the manifestation of salvation on a continual basis in the life of a Christian.

Questions and Answers

1. **What is the difference between receiving salvation and maintaining salvation? (Section 1C-D; Page 51)**

   Receiving Salvation
   - One believes and confesses Jesus Christ.
   - Jesus Christ is Lord (sole authority) in a Christian's life.
   - Salvation is freely given and does not have to be earned.

   Maintaining Salvation
   Nurturing the gift of salvation so that the gift remains in perpetual (continuous) existence through:
   - Getting planted in a local church
   - Prayer and Bible study
   - Maintaining a godly atmosphere

2. **Philippians 2:12-13 (NLT) says,** __Work__ __hard__ **to show the** __results__ **of your** __salvation__, __obeying__ **God with** __deep__ __reverence__ **and** __fear__. **For God is** __working__ **in you** __giving__ **you the** __desire__ **and the** __power__ **to** __do__ **what** __pleases__ __him__. **(Section 1F:1b; Page 51)**

3. **Explain what *work out* means in Philippians 2:12-13. (Section 2F:2b-c; Page 51)**

   The word *work* in the context of this Scripture does not indicate that salvation is obtained through merited works. *Work* is used in the context of intentional effort. An intentional effort to nurture and maintain your gift of salvation brings about or results in the manifestation of salvation on a continual basis in the life of a Christian.

TRANSFORMATION: LEADER EDITION

Self-Check

---

4. What areas in your life are you working on so that it reflects the results of salvation? Include how you are working (Page 52).

Example 1
Finances: budgeting, saving, debt elimination
- Budgeting - Get samples of a budget and create one using current income and expenditures.
- Saving – Eliminate unnecessary spending based on the budget and place those funds into a savings account.
- Debt Elimination – Make a list of all debts including pay off balances. Include in budget.

Example 2
Addiction
- The root of addiction is rebellion. Make an assessment to evaluate where obedience to God has not been active.
- Remove people, places, and things that contribute to the addiction or serve as triggers.
- Attend a church that teaches the uncompromised Word of God and get planted.
- Find someone that will provide accountability.

*Refer to the **Group Leader Suggestions** listed in the **How to Use Transformation Leader Edition** section located at the beginning of the curriculum.*

II. CHRISTIANS AND SINNERS

A. The title Christian was given to the disciples of Jesus in the city of Antioch as stated in Acts 11:26 **(53)**.

    1. Christian is derived from the Greek word *Christianos* meaning a follower of Christ.[4]

    2. Therefore, a Christian is one who believes in the Father, Son, and Holy Spirit; has received salvation; and displays behavior that reflects the godly standards set forth in the Bible.

B. The title of sinner refers to one who consistently engages in sinful behavior. Sin is behavior that contradicts the Word of God **(53)**.

C. What is the difference between those who live a life of sin and a Christian who happens to sin **(53)**?

    1. Individuals who live a life of sin are sinners because they consistently engage in a sinful lifestyle.

    2. A true Christian is not a sinner because they do not consistently engage in a sinful lifestyle.

    3. Therefore, the phrase "I am a sinner saved by grace" is incorrect.

        a. It should be stated, "I was a sinner; now I am saved by grace."

        b. *What shall we say then? Shall we continue in sin that grace may abound? Certainly not! How shall we who died to sin live any longer in it?*   ROMANS 6:1-2

D. If a Christian happens to sin, it is appropriate to ask for forgiveness and repent. It does not mean that person is no longer saved **(53)**.

    1. Forgiveness does not release the Christian from the responsibility of working on his or her weak areas.

    2. It is a command for Christians to work out their soul salvation with fear and trembling (Philippians 2:12-13).

    3. If a sinner desires to become a Christian, he or she must receive salvation as stated in chapter 1.

E. Read the additional Scriptures taken from the Amplified Bible. These specific verses provide clarity and insight regarding the difference between a Christian and a sinner **(53-56)**:

1. And when Jesus heard it, He said to them, Those who are strong and well have no need of a physician, but those who are weak and sick; I came not to call the righteous ones to repentance, but sinners (the erring ones and all those not free from sin). MARK 2:17

2. [16] But I say, walk and live [habitually] in the [Holy] Spirit [responsive to and controlled and guided by the Spirit]; then you will certainly not gratify the cravings and desires of the flesh (of human nature without God). [17] For the desires of the flesh are opposed to the [Holy] Spirit, and the [desires of the] Spirit are opposed to the flesh (godless human nature); for these are antagonistic to each other [continually withstanding and in conflict with each other], so that you are not free but are prevented from doing what you desire to do. [18] But if you are guided (led) by the [Holy] Spirit, you are not subject to the Law.

   [19] Now the doings (practices) of the flesh are clear (obvious): they are immorality, impurity, indecency, [20] idolatry, sorcery, enmity, strife, jealousy, anger (ill temper), selfishness, divisions (dissensions), party spirit (factions, sects with peculiar opinions, heresies), [21] envy, drunkenness, carousing, and the like. I warn you beforehand, just as I did previously, that those who do such things shall not inherit the kingdom of God.

   [22] But the fruit of the [Holy] Spirit [the work which His presence within accomplishes] is love, joy (gladness), peace, patience (an even temper, forbearance), kindness, goodness (benevolence), faithfulness, [23] gentleness (meekness, humility), self-control (self-restraint, continence). Against such things there is no law [that can bring a charge].

   [24] And those who belong to Christ Jesus (the Messiah) have crucified the flesh (the godless human nature) with its passions and appetites and desires. [25] If we live by the [Holy] Spirit, let us also walk by the Spirit. [If by the Holy Spirit we have our life in God, let us go forward walking in line, our conduct controlled by the Spirit.] GALATIANS 5:16-25

3. *But as He who called you is holy, you also be holy in all your conduct, because it is written, "Be holy, for I am holy."* 1 PETER 1:15-16

4. *Now, "If the righteous one is scarcely saved, where will the ungodly and the sinner appear?"* 1 PETER 4:18

5. *⁶No one who abides in Him [who lives and remains in communion with and in obedience to Him—deliberately, knowingly, and habitually] commits (practices) sin. No one who [habitually] sins has either seen or known Him [recognized, perceived, or understood Him, or has had an experiential acquaintance with Him].*

⁷ Boys (lads), let no one deceive and lead you astray. He who practices righteousness [who is upright, conforming to the divine will in purpose, thought, and action, living a consistently conscientious life] is righteous, even as He is righteous.

⁸ [But] he who commits sin [who practices evildoing] is of the devil [takes his character from the evil one], for the devil has sinned (violated the divine law) from the beginning. The reason the Son of God was made manifest (visible) was to undo (destroy, loosen, and dissolve) the works the devil [has done].

⁹ No one born (begotten) of God [deliberately, knowingly, and habitually] practices sin, for God's nature abides in him [His principle of life, the divine seed, remains permanently within him]; and he cannot practice sinning because he is born (begotten) of God.

¹⁰ By this it is made clear who take their nature from God and are His children and who take their nature from the devil and are his children: no one who does not practice righteousness [who does not conform to God's will in purpose, thought, and action] is of God; neither is anyone who does not love his brother (his fellow believer in Christ).

1 JOHN 3:6-10, V.9 EMPHASIS ADDED

6. *For the [true] love of God is this: that we do His commands [keep His ordinances and are mindful of His precepts and teaching]. And these orders of His are not irksome (burdensome, oppressive, or grievous).*   1 JOHN 5:3

7. *All wrongdoing is sin, and there is sin which does not [involve] death [that may be repented of and forgiven].*   1 JOHN 5:17

Questions and Answers

1. **What is the difference between a Christian and a sinner (Page 56)?**
   - A Christian is one who believes in the Father, Son, and Holy Spirit; has received salvation; and displays behavior that reflects the godly standards set forth in the Bible. **(Section IIA:2)**
   - The title of sinner refers to one who consistently engages in sinful behavior. **(Section IIB)**

2. **Why is the phrase "I am a sinner saved by grace" incorrect? (Section IIC:2-3a; Page 56)**

   A true Christian is not a sinner because they do not sin all the time. Therefore, the phrase "I am a sinner saved by grace" is incorrect. It should be stated, "I was a sinner, now I am saved by grace."

3. **List at least two Scriptures that prove an individual cannot be both a Christian and a sinner. (Section IIE; Page 56)**

   Mark 2:17; Galatians 5:16-25; 1 Peter 1:15-16; 1 Peter 4:18; 1 John 3:6-10; 1 John 5:17

Self-Check

1. Assess your lifestyle. Based upon the verses listed in this section, are you a Christian or a sinner (Page 57)?

2. Using the answer you provided in the previous question, list at least two actions in which you consistently engage to prove your answer to be an accurate assessment. What Scriptures can you find to prove that the actions you listed are those of a Christian or a sinner (Page 57)?

*Refer to the **Group Leader Suggestions** listed in the **How to Use Transformation Leader Edition** section located at the beginning of the curriculum.*

III. REPENTANCE

A. 1 John 1:9 says, *"If we confess our sins, He is faithful and just to forgive us our sins and to cleanse us from all unrighteousness."* Once sin has been confessed, and forgiveness has been obtained, repentance must be put into action. Before we go any further with repentance, let us review forgiveness **(58)**.

1. Forgiveness grants release from payment or indebtedness.
   a. When Jesus stated that *"He is faithful and just to forgive us our sins"* (1 John 1:9), it means that our sins are not held against us. He has wiped the slate clean. Hallelujah!
   b. Once forgiveness is obtained, a ***conscious decision*** must be made to no longer sin.
   c. Christians are to live a life of repentance. We should always stay in a mode of making decisions to follow Christ.

B. Repentance is a 1) **changed mind to do the will of God** 2) **accompanied with the appropriate actions** (actions that are aligned with the Word of God) (Romans 12:1-2) **(58)**.

1. Mark 2:17 says, *"Those who are well have no need of a physician, but those who are sick. I did not come to call the righteous, but sinners, to repentance."*
   a. In this passage of Scripture, Jesus is making the point that the righteous (those in right relationship with Him) do not need to repent. They have already turned away from sin and are now in proper relationship with God.
   b. It is the sinner He is calling to repentance.

C. Below is a concise explanation of forgiveness and repentance **(58)**.

1. *Forgiveness* is God's responsibility. All one has to do is ask and receive.
2. *Repentance* is the individual's responsibility to change their mindset to do the will of God *accompanied with appropriate actions*.

D. **Example of Repentance (Page 58-59)**

Hi, my name is Todd. Before I received salvation I had a bad habit of using profanity, especially when I became angry. I immediately asked God for forgiveness in this area but still struggled with using profanity. When I learned of repentance in my Christian Living class at church, I learned that I had to do more than just ask for forgiveness. I learned that I can receive forgiveness when I ask, but I had to put actions in place and make a decision to turn away from sin. I learned that repentance is a changed mind to do the will of God accompanied with the appropriate actions. I found Scripture verses that specifically dealt with godly communication. Ephesians 4:29 is one of my favorites! Studying and confessing these Scriptures helped me change my mindset about profanity and adopt godly communication.

Second, I made a decision to ask my friends and coworkers not to use profanity in my presence. I also eliminated music, television shows, and movies that contained profanity. I noticed after a few weeks I was no longer using profanity.

Using the Scriptures to change my mind and putting a plan into action helped me achieve true deliverance. I now notice that I am able to edify and encourage others in the way of the Lord. To God be all the glory!

This short story illustrates the changes Todd made in his life to ensure that he would not fall back into the ungodly behavior of using profanity. *God does not forgive with the intention that we return to sinful behavior. *This shaded portion is not included in the Q & A section. However, the leader should place emphasis on this point.*

E. Let's review Todd's process of deliverance. Again, repentance is *a changed mind to do the will of God with appropriate actions* **(59-60).**

1. Todd stated that he attended his Christian Living class. It is vitally important that Christians stay connected to God through personal prayer and study time and becoming planted in a local church. This cannot be stated enough! Todd

consistently attended church.

2. Second, Todd changed his mindset about profanity by using the Word of God. He found Scripture verses for his specific problem. When going through the process of deliverance, it is vitally important to find verses that edify your spirit to do the opposite of the behavior that is not glorifying God. In this case, Todd needed to adopt godly communication; therefore, he found verses pertaining to this area.

3. Third, Todd had to take some action to stop exposing himself to profanity. This resulted in changing conversation styles and entertainment choices. When changing your lifestyle, it is also important to acknowledge when it is necessary to change the company you keep. This may involve releasing some friends, family, and other relationships. If a relationship is pushing you away from God, then it is time to make a change.

4. Last, Todd was able to be a witness to encourage and edify others in the way of the Lord.

F. Always remember that repentance has two parts: 1) a **changed mind** to obey the Word of God with 2) **appropriate actions** (actions that match your decision to obey the Word of God). Mark 2:17 proves that you cannot be saved and continue to sin **(60)**.
  1. Living a life of sin takes you out of right relationship (righteousness) with God.
  2. Once you are out of relationship you have lost your place in the kingdom of God.
  3. Repentance is necessary to restore a right relationship with God, as well as restoration to your rightful place in the kingdom of God (Luke 15:11-31).
  4. This puts to rest the incorrect belief of "once saved, always saved" (1 Peter 4:18). Scripture does not prove that doctrine to be accurate.
  5. Repentance shows gratitude to God for the gift of salvation and forgiveness given to us, which we do not deserve on our own merit (Luke 15:19-31).

G. *For the kind of sorrow God wants us to experience leads us away from sin and results in salvation. There's no regret for that kind of sorrow. But worldly sorrow, which lacks repentance, results in spiritual death.* 2 CORINTHIANS 7:10

Questions and Answers

1. **List the two parts of repentance (Section IIIB; Page 61):**
   - A **changed mind** to do the will of God

   accompanied with

   - **Appropriate Actions** (actions that are aligned with the Word of God).

2. **What scriptures support the actions of repentance? (Section IIIA:B1; Page 61)**
   1 John 1:9, Mark 2:17

3. **What is the difference between forgiveness and repentance? (Section IIIC; Page 61)**
   - *Forgiveness* is God's responsibility. All one has to do is ask and receive.

   - *Repentance* is the individual's responsibility to change their mindset to do the will of God *accompanied with appropriate actions*.

4. **What did Todd *do* to get a "changed mind to do the will of God" (the first part of repentance)? (Section IIIE:1-2; Page 61)**
   - He attended Christian Living Class at his church.
   - Todd found scriptures that specifically dealt with Godly communication (Ephesians 4:29).

5. **What *actions* did Todd display with the second part of repentance (accompanying actions)? (Section IIIE:3; Page 61)**
   - Todd asked his friends and co-workers not to use profanity in his presence.
   - He eliminated music, television shows, and movies which contained profanity.

   Refer to the last two paragraphs in section IIID.

 Self-Check

1. **Identify areas in your life in which you need to exemplify repentance. For each area list the following (Page 62):**

    - **Changed Mind** – Find Scriptures that address your area of need (a topical Bible will help with this). Remember that you need to do the opposite of the sin. Find verses that support the behavior or goal you are striving to achieve.
      Example - Anger, Ephesians 4:26

    - **Accompanying actions to support a changed mind** – List the actions that need to be implemented to facilitate full repentance.
      Example - Anger: 1) Stop and count to ten. 2) Pray before responding. 3) Discontinue spending time with people who trigger the anger.

*Refer to the **Group Leader Suggestions** listed in the **How to Use Transformation Leader Edition** section located at the beginning of the curriculum.*

IV. WHAT IS GRACE?

A. Grace is unmerited supernatural assistance given to humans for their regeneration (a life reflecting the fruit of salvation) and sanctification (set apart for holiness).
  1. Unmerited means it was given without having to be earned.

B. Pastor Dennis Clark provides an excellent definition of grace:
Grace is the personal presence of Jesus enabling and empowering Christians to be and to do, ALL that He called you to be and ALL that He called you to do.5

C. Grace does not excuse sin but empowers the Christian to come out of sin, repent, and bear Godly fruit.

D. *For by **grace** you have been saved through faith, and that not of yourselves; it is the gift of God, not of works, lest anyone should boast. For we are His workmanship, created in Christ Jesus for **good works**, which God prepared beforehand that we should walk in them."*

EPHESIANS 2:8-10

E. Christians are saved by God's grace and not by works or actions. In other words, we cannot do anything to earn salvation. It has been freely given; therefore, we are to receive freely.

  1. Ephesians 2:8-10 states that a person's works (actions and behaviors) cannot save; however, it does not excuse the requirement that a Christian should exemplify Christ-like behavior.
  2. In Ephesians 2:10, Paul states, *"We are His workmanship, created in Christ Jesus for good works which God prepared beforehand that we should walk in them."*
  3. This proves that grace is given to supernaturally assist a Christian to obey the commandments of Christ displaying good works (godly actions and behavior).

TRANSFORMATION: LEADER EDITION

Questions and Answers

1. **What is grace? (Section IVB; Page 64)**

   Grace is the __personal__ __presence__ **of Jesus** __enabling__ **and** __empowering__ **Christians to** __be__ **and to** __do__ **, ALL that He** __called__ **you to** __be__ **, and ALL that He** __called__ **you to** __do__ **.**

2. What was your understanding of grace prior to this study (Page 64)?

Self-Check

3. Describe what *grace* should look like in your life as a Christian (Page 64).

*Refer to the **Group Leader Suggestions** listed in the **How to Use Transformation Leader Edition** section located at the beginning of the curriculum.*

184

V. FASTING

A. What is fasting (65)?

Fasting is abstaining from food for a specific amount of time.

B. What is the purpose of fasting (65)?

Fasting develops a closer, stronger, and more intimate relationship with God.

C. How does fasting strengthen a relationship with God (65)?

1. Fasting holistically humbles one (spirit, soul, and body) before God (*Psalm 35:13*).
2. Fasting empties oneself to be refilled with God (*John 3:30-31*).
3. Fasting re-centers the relationship with God (*Proverbs 3:5-6*).
4. Fasting chastens (corrects) bringing one into complete obedience (*Psalm 69:10; Romans 8:5*).
5. Fasting crucifies the appetite creating a dependence on God (*Galatians 5:24*).

D. What are the results of fasting (65)?

1. Undistracted earnestness (seriousness) towards God both during and after fasting (*Luke 9:23; 1 Corinthians 7:5*)
2. Obedience (*Isaiah 58:6*)
3. Victory over temptation, addiction, and oppression (*Luke 4: 1-13*)
4. Power over demonic spirits (*Matthew 17:14-21*)
5. Develops faith and crucifies unbelief (doubt) (*Matthew 17:19-21*)
6. Empowers prayer (*Matthew 4:1-11, 17:14-21*)
7. Physical healing (*Isaiah 58:8*)

E. When should a Christian fast (66)?

1. When prompted by the Holy Spirit (*Isaiah 58:6*)
2. In need (*Ezra 8:21*)
3. Danger (*Esther 4*)

4. Worried (*Daniel 6:18-23*)

5. In trouble (*Acts 27:9, 33*)

6. Spiritual conflict (*Matthew 4:1-11*)

7. Desperate in prayer (*Acts 9*)

F. Types of Fast (66)

1. Liquid Fast

2. Vegetarian Fast – Abstinence of animal, artificially flavored, and processed foods.

3. Individual Meal Fast – Abstinence from specific meals (breakfast, lunch, or dinner).

G. Fasting and Praying (66)

1. Fasting should always be accompanied with prayer.

2. Fasting requires dependence on God to endure.

3. Maintaining a strong prayer life when fasting strengthens the connection with God; therefore, strengthening faith.

4. This guarantees that God will provide whatever is needed to endure the time of fasting.

5. It is the element of prayer coupled with fasting that brings about supernatural results.

6. Fasting without prayer is nothing more than abstaining from food. *See Matthew 17:14-21.*

H. Fasting with a Pure Motive (66)

1. Fasting should be done privately.

2. It should not be done to flaunt how spiritual or dedicated one is to God.

3. It should earnestly be done so that God receives the glory by the fruit it bears in the life of a Christian. *See Matthew 6:16-18 and Luke 18:11-13.*

I. **Fasting Best Practices (66-67)**

There are some practices that should be exemplified to obtain the best results from the fasting period. These practices will eliminate distractions so that one can give complete attention to the Lord.

1. Eliminate entertainment, including TV, music, gaming devices, shopping, movies, or anything that serves the purpose of entertaining. This best practice should be observed both at home and in motor vehicles. This time can be spent in prayer, meditation, or study. Electronic devices such as an iPod or mp3 player are recommended to listen to audio versions of the Bible/Scriptures and sermons or teachings.

2. Eliminate the use of cell phones and any other handheld device unless it is for work or to keep in touch with family in the event of an emergency.

3. Refrain from social media unless it is required for work purposes.

4. Incorporate family Bible study if this is not already in practice.

5. Refrain from eating out if you are on a modified meal fast. It eliminates distractions, temptations, and exposure to carnal entertainment. This is a great opportunity to learn how to prepare healthy entrees to maintain ultimate health for the work of the Kingdom.

6. If possible, turn off your electronic devices during prayer and study time. If this is not possible for work or family reasons, set up special rings or alerts to receive important calls.

7. See the following Scriptures to help maintain focus on God: *Psalm 119:1-3; Proverbs 5:1-2; Isaiah 50:7, 58:1-14; Philippians 4:8; 1 Peter 5:8.*

Questions and Answers

1. **State the purpose of fasting in your own words. (Section VB; Page 68)**

    Fasting develops a closer, stronger, and more intimate relationship with God.

2. **List at least three of the five ways fasting strengthens a relationship with God.**

    (Section VC; Page 68)
    - Fasting holistically humbles one (spirit, soul, and body) before God.
    - Fasting empties oneself to be refilled with God.
    - Fasting re-centers the relationship with God.
    - Fasting chastens (corrects) bringing one into complete obedience.
    - Fasting crucifies the appetite creating a dependence on God.

3. **List at least four of the seven results of fasting. (Section VD; Page 68)**
    - Undistracted earnestness (seriousness) towards God both during and after fasting
    - Obedience
    - Victory over temptation, addiction, and oppression
    - Power over demonic spirits
    - Develops faith and crucifies unbelief (doubt)
    - Empowers prayer
    - Physical healing

4. **List four of the seven occasions in which a Christian should fast.**

    (Section VE; Page 68)
    - When prompted by the Holy Spirit
    - In need
    - Danger
    - Worried
    - In trouble
    - Spiritual conflict
    - Desperate in prayer

5. **Why is prayer necessary during fasting? (Section VG:3; Page 68)**

    Maintaining a strong prayer life when fasting strengthens the connection with God; therefore, strengthening faith.

6. **List four of the seven Fasting Best Practices. (Section VI; Page 68)**
    - Eliminate entertainment, including TV, music, gaming devices, shopping, movies, or anything that serves the purpose of entertaining.
    - Eliminate the use of cell phones and any other handheld device unless it is for work or to keep in touch with family in the event of an emergency.
    - Refrain from social media unless it is required for work purposes.
    - Incorporate family Bible study if this is not already in practice.
    - Refrain from eating out if you are on a modified meal fast.
    - Turn off your electronic devices during prayer and study time.
    - See the following Scriptures to help maintain focus on God: *Psalm 119:1-3; Proverbs 5:1-2; Isaiah 50:7, 58:1-14; Philippians 4:8; 1 Peter 5:8.*

Questions and Answers

7. **Assess your previous fasting experiences. Did you experience any of the results listed in this section? How so (Page 69)?**

8. **What Fasting Best Practices will you implement on your next fast that you have not previously done (Page 69)?**

Refer to the **Group Leader Suggestions** *listed in the* **How to Use Transformation Leader Edition** *section located at the beginning of the curriculum.*

TRANSFORMATION: LEADER EDITION

VI. WHAT IF I STILL HAVE ISSUES AFTER I BECOME A CHRISTIAN?

A. All Christians will have areas in their lives in which they may struggle. No one should ever be ashamed of having issues **(70)**.

B. Grace empowers the Christian to overcome every struggle and issue in life **(70)**.
1. Are your issues defeating you?
2. Philippians 2:12-13 states, *"Work out your own salvation with fear and trembling; for it is God who works in you both to will and to do for His good pleasure."*

C. The following are some questions to help determine if you are ***working out your soul salvation*** **(70)**.
1. Place a "Y" for yes or "N" for no next to each question below.
    - Have you made up your mind to live like a Christian? _____
    - Have you submitted your issues to the Lord? _____
    - Do you have ***corresponding actions*** that will bring about deliverance in the area(s) in which you are experiencing difficulty? _____
    - Are you actively engaged in the Word finding verses to address your issues? _____
    - Do you have other strong Christians holding you accountable? _____
    - Are you planted and consistently attending a church that is teaching the uncompromised Word of God? _____
2. If the answer is yes to these questions, salvation is being worked out.
3. If some or all of the answers were no, make the necessary steps to activate the actions in the questions so that those answers become yes.

D. God knows His children will have issues **(70)**.
1. That is why He said in Hebrews 4:16, *"Let us therefore come boldly to the throne of grace, that we may obtain mercy and find grace to help in time of need."*
2. Remember that you are saved by grace. This supernatural grace enables and

empowers you to be what God has called you to be and do what He has commanded. You can overcome your issues!

3. To activate this grace (the personal presence of Jesus), you have to feed and maintain your spirit with the Word of God.

4. Refer to "The Seven Steps to Maintaining Salvation" at the end of this chapter for more detail.

E. A relationship with Christ has to be maintained. In other words, what you say and what you do must match. This is proven in the following Scriptures taken from the New King James Version **(71)**:

1. *"Not everyone who says to Me, 'Lord, Lord,' shall enter the kingdom of heaven, but he who does the will of My Father in heaven. Many will say to Me in that day, 'Lord, Lord, have we not prophesied in Your name, cast out demons in Your name, and done many wonders in Your name?' And then I will declare to them, 'I never knew you; depart from Me, you who practice lawlessness!'"* MATTHEW 7:21-23

2. *Well then, should we keep on sinning so that God can show us more and more of his wonderful grace? Of course not! Since we have died to sin, how can we continue to live in it? Or have you forgotten that when we were joined with Christ Jesus in baptism we joined him in his death? For we died and were buried with Christ by baptism. And just as Christ was raised from the dead by the glorious power of the Father, now we also may live new lives . . . Well then, since God's grace has set us free from the law, does that mean we can go on sinning? Of course not!* ROMANS 6:1-4, 15, NLT

3. *Therefore, if anyone is in Christ, he is a new creation; old things have passed away; behold, all things have become new.* 2 CORINTHIANS 5:17

4. *Do not be unequally yoked together with unbelievers. For what fellowship has righteousness with lawlessness? And what communion has light with darkness? And what accord has Christ with Belial? Or what part has a believer with an unbeliever? And what agreement*

has the temple of God with idols? For you are the temple of the living God. As God has said, "I will dwell in them and walk among them. I will be their God, and they shall be My people." Therefore, "Come out from among them and be separate," says the Lord. "Do not touch what is unclean, and I will receive you. I will be a Father to you, and you shall be My sons and daughters," says the Lord Almighty. 2 CORINTHIANS 6:14-18

5. *Therefore, my beloved, as you have always obeyed, not as in my presence only, but now much more in my absence, work out your own salvation with fear and trembling; for it is God who works in you both to will and to do for His good pleasure.* PHILIPPIANS 2:12-13

6. *But as He who called you is holy, you also be holy in all your conduct, because it is written, "Be holy, for I am holy."* 1 PETER 1:15-16

7. *Now, "If the righteous one is scarcely saved, where will the ungodly and the sinner appear?"* 1 PETER 4:18

Self-Check

1. Select at least three Scriptures that support the maintaining of salvation. (Section VIE; Page 72)

2. Explain why you chose those particular verses (Page 72).

*Refer to the **Group Leader Suggestions** listed in the **How to Use Transformation Leader Edition** section located at the beginning of the curriculum.*

VII. SEVEN STEPS TO MAINTAIN SALVATION

Listed below are seven steps, if consistently implemented, will help you to maintain your salvation.

Step 1
Get planted in a Bible-based, Holy Spirit-filled church (Psalm 92:12-14). This is the most critical step after receiving salvation. Getting planted in an uncompromising Word-based church will provide accountability and teaching of the Word of God. Attending church provides the opportunity to be around other Christians. The pastor or spiritual leader of a congregation watches for the souls of the parishioners, challenges their spiritual growth, and creates opportunities to develop gifts and talents. It is also essential not to allow situations or individuals to create a hindrance to your church connection.

Step 2
Read the Bible and pray every day (Matthew 4:4; Hebrews 4:16). Begin by studying and reviewing the sermons and teachings taught during Sunday worship, Bible study, Sunday school, and/or small group. Take an assessment of the areas that present difficulties. This could be finances, addiction, hanging around the wrong people, lying, cursing, laziness, or any other issue. Find Scriptures that address those areas and confess them daily until godly results are evident. A study Bible and topical Bible should be acquired to assist in effective study habits.

Step 3
Hang around other strong Christians (Hebrews 10:24-25). Make it a habit to be surrounded by other victorious Christians that will provide encouragement, strength, and accountability.

Step 4

Maintain a godly atmosphere (2 Corinthians 6:14). Prohibit anything that does not bring glory to God from entering the eye and ear gates. This includes music, movies, and television programs that glorify sinful behavior. Sinful behavior can be any actions that contradict the Word of God. In addition, do not become fearful to separate from individuals who are consistently negative and distract from the things of God.

Step 5

Get filled with the Holy Spirit (Acts 2:4). The Holy Spirit is the Spirit of God living inside every believer. The Holy Spirit is the third person of the Trinity and is the power source for the Christian. What separates Christianity from other religions is that Christians can have the power of the true and living God residing within. The power of the Holy Spirit gives us the supernatural ability to live victoriously in Christ and take authority over the flesh. Every Christian should desire to be filled with the Holy Spirit (also referred to as the baptism of the Holy Spirit). The Holy Spirit is given by simply asking to be filled. The evidence that one has received the infilling of the Holy Spirit is a heavenly utterance, commonly known as tongues. Refer to Acts 2 when the disciples were filled with the Holy Spirit. Chapter 5 explains the Holy Spirit in detail.

Step 6

Walk in the fruit of the Spirit (Galatians 5:16-26). The fruit of the Spirit has to do with Christian character. Salvation is for the whole person: spirit, soul, and body. Christians should walk in integrity displaying godly character. There are nine characteristics and manifestations of the fruit of the Spirit: love, joy, peace, patience, kindness, goodness, faithfulness, gentleness, and self-control.

Step 7

Witness. Jesus gives the disciples a command in Mark 16:15 to "preach the gospel to every creature." This is the great commission of the church of Jesus Christ. Christians are to tell others about the saving grace of Jesus Christ. The behavior and character of Christians should be the first witness. Second, Christians should engage in witnessing as the Holy Spirit dictates. This can be done through praying for others, sharing your testimony, encouraging and edifying through Scripture, and compelling others to come to Christ. Incorporate evangelism into your prayer life. Ask God to send you to individuals who need to hear about Christ.

CHAPTER 4

THE TRINITY: FATHER, SON, AND HOLY SPIRIT

I. WHO IS THE TRINITY?

A. The Trinity is comprised of the Father, the Son, and the Holy Spirit. They are all three distinct persons, with three distinct functions; yet they are one God (Isaiah 43:10, 44:6, 45:14, 18, 21-22) **(79)**.

1. They are co-equal, co-eternal, and co-powerful.
2. It is argued that the Trinity is not biblical because the actual word *trinity* is not in the Bible.
3. Trinity is derived from the Latin word *trinitas* which is translated as "the number three or triad".[6]

B. The Trinity is best explained using the example of a family unit **(79)**.

1. In a family, there is a father, a mother, and usually at least one child.
2. They are one family but have different functions: Robert Jones (father, husband), Sarah Jones (wife, mother), Chad Jones (son, brother), Tracy Jones (daughter, sister).
3. They all come from the same family but are one family unit. It is the same with the Trinity.

C. All three are a family unit that comes out of the source of God **(79)**.

1. God is the family unit:
   a. 1) God the Father: the creator and the source of everything.
   b. 2) God the Son (Jesus): Jesus comes from God and is the mediator between God and mankind. We are made righteous through Him.
   c. 3) God the Holy Spirit: the Spirit of God that lives on the inside of a Christian. He is the element that empowers Christians to carry out the mission of the church.

D. If each person of the Trinity were named according to societal norm for first and last names, they would be named as such: the God family: Father (first name) God (last name), Jesus God (the Son of God), Holy Spirit God. Three functions, but one family unit **(79)**.

E. Another example would be a grocery store chain. For the sake of this example the chain is Manna Bread Grocery **(80)**.
1. Manna Bread Grocery is the corporation, but stores are located in various places.
2. Though there may be various locations they are separate entities bearing the name Manna Bread Grocery.
3. Each store serves its function where it is located—one entity with many locations.

II. FUNCTION OF EACH PERSON OF THE TRINITY

This section will explain the designated purpose of the Father, Son, and the Holy Spirit.

A. The Function of the Father
Everything is sent out through the Father. He is the creator of everything.
See Genesis 1:1,26 and Isaiah 42:5,45:18.

B. The Function of the Son
The Son (Jesus Christ) is the receiver of the Father's authority and the mediator between God and man. Through His sacrifice on the cross we are declared righteous.
1. Jesus' blood shed on the cross removes the guilt and punishment of our sins.
2. His sacrifice provides salvation.
3. Those who believe and confess Jesus as Lord have the opportunity to be in right relationship (righteousness) and gain a new life in Jesus Christ. *See John 6:37-40,12:45,14:16; Colossians 1:16-19; and 1 Timothy 2:5.*

C. The Function of the Holy Spirit

The Holy Spirit is in partnership with the Father and Son to help carry out the mission of the church.

1. He is the one who empowers, teaches, leads, guides, and comforts. He is the power source, the anointing. *See John 16:7,13 and Acts 1:8.*

III. ADDITIONAL SCRIPTURAL REFERENCES

A. It must be understood that though the Father, Son, and Holy Spirit have different functions there is no hierarchy. They operate in the power of agreement. Below are additional scriptural references about the Trinity.

1. **The Father, Son, and the Holy Spirit are referred to as God.**
    Philippians 1:2; Colossians 2:9; Acts 5:3-5

2. **The Father, Son, and the Holy Spirit are referred to as Creator**
    Isaiah 64:8; John 1:3; Colossians 1:15-17; Job 26:13, 33:4

Questions and Answers

1. **Who is the Trinity? (Section IA; Page 82)**

    The Trinity is comprised of the Father, Son, and the Holy Spirit. They are all three distinct persons, with three distinct functions, yet they are one God (Isaiah 43:10; 44:6; 45:14,18, 21, 22).

2. **Provide at least one practical example of the Trinity stated in this chapter. Explain in your own words. (Sections IB or IE; Page 82)**
    - The Trinity is best explained using the example of a family unit. In a family there is a father, a mother, and at least a child.
    - If each person of the Trinity were named according to societal norm for first and last names, they would be named as such: The God Family: Father (first name) God (last name), Jesus God (the Son of God), Holy Spirit God.
    - Another example would be a grocery store chain. For the sake of this example the chain is Manna Bread Grocery. Though there may be various locations they are separate entities bearing the name Manna Bread Grocery.

3. **State the function of the Father, Son, and Holy Spirit. (Page 82)**
    - **Function of the Father:** Everything is sent out through Him. The creator of everything. (Genesis 1:1,26 ; Isaiah 42:5,45:18) **(Section IIA)**

    - **Function of the Son:** The Son (Jesus Christ) is the receiver of the Father's authority and the mediator between God and man. Through His sacrifice on the cross we are declared righteous. **(Section IIB)**

    - **Function of the Holy Spirit:** The Holy Spirit is in partnership with Jesus to help carry out the mission of the church. He is the one who empowers, teaches, leads, guides, and comforts. He is the power source, the anointing. **(Section IIC)**

CHAPTER 5

THE HOLY SPIRIT

I. WHO IS THE HOLY SPIRIT?

A. He is the Spirit of God who lives on the inside of the Christian.
   1. The Holy Spirit is not an it, but a person (Acts 13:2).
   2. He is the power source. He is the Comforter, Teacher, Guide, and Helper (John 14:26, 16:13).
   3. Every Christian should desire to have the baptism of the Holy Spirit.
      a. It is an overflow of God's Spirit (John 7:38).
      b. It is like having a Cadillac Escalade fully loaded. The Holy Spirit fully loads the Christian, providing extra benefits and an advantage over the enemy.
   4. These extra benefits include:
      a. The ability to pray God's perfect will (Romans 8:26)
      b. Operation in the gifts of the Spirit (chapter 6)
      c. Operation in supernatural power (Mark 16:16-17)

B. He is supernatural in existence.
   1. Supernatural is anything that occurs beyond natural or human abilities.
   2. The power that comes with the Holy Spirit is beyond human ability.
   3. This is the same power that endowed Jesus when He worked miracles, signs, and wonders.
   4. This supernatural power that enabled Jesus to do signs and wonders was not solely for Jesus.
      a. John 14:12 states, *"Most assuredly, I say to you, he who believes in Me, the works that I do he will do also; and greater works than these he will do, because I go to My Father."*
      b. In John 16, Jesus speaks of sending the Holy Spirit (Helper) to "guide you into all truth" (v. 13).

C. The Holy Spirit also will empower the Christian to endure, successfully handle, and overcome everyday issues that occur in life.
  1. This supernatural power is for every Christian who will receive it.
  2. It is the same power Jesus spoke about in Acts 1:8 before ascending into heaven.
  3. This is the same power that filled the apostles in the upper room in Acts 2:4. *See Luke 12:12; John 7:39, 14:26, 16:13; Romans 8:14,16; 1 Corinthians 2:10-11; 1 Corinthians 2:13; and Galatians 5:18.*

II. THE FUNCTION OF THE HOLY SPIRIT

A. The Holy Spirit is in partnership with God the Father and God the Son to help carry out the mission of the church.

B. He is the one who empowers, teaches, leads, guides, and comforts (Acts 1:8; Luke 12:12; John 14:26, 16:13).

C. The Holy Spirit is the intercessor praying the perfect will of the Father at all times (Romans 8:26). He is the power source, the anointing (Acts 1:8).

III. BAPTISM OF THE HOLY SPIRIT

A. The baptism of the Holy Spirit occurs when a Christian receives an overflow of God's Spirit (John 4:13-14, 7:38). The baptism of the Holy Spirit (also referred to as being filled with the Spirit) is evident through speaking in tongues.
  1. Tongues are a heavenly language that only God can understand.
  2. It is the Spirit of God praying His perfect will.
  3. As stated at the beginning of this chapter, every Christian should desire to have the baptism of the Holy Spirit. It is an overflow of God's Spirit (John 7:38). It is like having a luxury car fully loaded.

B. All a Christian has to do is simply ask, and he or she will become filled with His Spirit.
  1. The baptism of the Holy Spirit can also be received through the laying on of hands.
  2. However, the laying on of hands does not make a person speak in tongues. It is simply a point of contact.

C. Once a Christian has been filled with the Holy Spirit, he or she should ask God for the *gift of tongues* so he or she can speak at any time (See Chapter 6 for more details). Examples of believers being filled with the Holy Spirit are found in the following verses: Acts 8:14-17, 9:17, 10:44, 15:8-9, 19:2-6.

IV. WHAT ARE "TONGUES"?

A. Tongues are a heavenly language only God can understand. It cannot be translated, only interpreted as the Holy Spirit reveals **(86)**.
  1. Receiving the baptism of the Holy Spirit will allow a Christian to receive a unique prayer language that can be spoken at any time.
  2. This is God praying His perfect will (Romans 8:26).

B. This prayer language can only be understood by God and cannot be translated. However, God can reveal at His discretion what is being prayed through interpretation **(86-87)**.
  1. Meaning, He will reveal in the native language what is being prayed through the person praying in tongues or another person.
  2. Chapter 6 explains the interpretation of tongues in detail.

C. This is extremely powerful because there can be no demonic interference with a Christian's prayers since they cannot be understood. Therefore, it is a guarantee that God's perfect will is being prayed in the heavenly language without hindrance or delay **(87)**.

V. WHEN CAN TONGUES (THE HEAVENLY LANGUAGE) BE SPOKEN?

A. Private Devotional Time (1 Corinthians 14:2, 4)
1. Tongues are direct contact with God and can be used in private devotional time.
2. Praying in tongues will strengthen, empower, comfort, and guide the Christian.
3. It is praying the perfect will of God. Therefore, prayers are rendered according to the perfect will of God.
4. There will be times in which God will reveal what is being prayed and times when He will not. Make certain to be obedient when God gives a prompting to pray in the Holy Spirit.

B. Corporate Worship and Prayer (1 Corinthians 14:2, 4)

Tongues can be spoken during corporate services during praise and worship segments of the service.

C. Tongues Draw the Unbeliever (Acts 2:4, 1 Corinthians 14:20-25)
1. God may use someone to speak in tongues or another foreign language to draw those who do not believe.
    a. This is done in a corporate gathering like a worship service. This can also occur in small group settings.
    b. There will always be an interpretation when God uses someone to speak in the heavenly language to address the church or group.
    c. An interpretation is necessary so parishioners will understand what has been spoken.
2. Remember, the Holy Spirit operates in an orderly fashion.
3. The Holy Spirit will also use someone to speak a message in a foreign language. This often occurs to spiritually edify those who speak that language.
    a. A biblical example would be the Day of Pentecost in Acts 2:5-8. The Holy Spirit was given, and the apostles spoke in other tongues.
    b. Those passing heard the gospel preached in their native language.

VI. BENEFITS OF SPEAKING IN TONGUES

A. Spiritual Edification

When you pray in tongues your spirit is praying, and it is in direct contact with God. God is Spirit; therefore, you are talking to Him in a supernatural language (1 Corinthians 14:2).

B. Praying the Perfect Will of God

1. Praying in tongues guarantees you are praying the perfect will of God (Romans 8:26).
2. Praying in tongues provides a double guarantee; you are praying the perfect will of God, and your prayers cannot be hindered because the devil cannot understand tongues.
3. Remember that tongues can only be interpreted, not translated (1 Corinthians 12:10).
4. You are also praying for the unknown. God will not reveal everything that is prayed in tongues. You have to trust that His perfect will is being done.

C. Stimulates Faith

1. Jude 20 says, *"But you, beloved, building up your most holy faith, praying in the Holy Spirit."*
2. It takes faith to pray in tongues because you do not know what you are saying.
3. You must trust God's Word that you are praying the perfect will of God (Romans 8:26) though you cannot understand with your human intellect.
4. If you can trust God in this area, it will help you to trust God in other areas of your life.
5. You are strengthening the principle of trusting God, affording you the ability to apply it in any area of your life and any situation.

D. Keeps One Free From Spiritual Contamination
1. Often times your spirit can be exposed to ungodly things beyond your control.
   a. This can be at work, shopping, at the gym, commercials on television, vulgar talk, and so on.
2. We are to be in this world, but not of it.
3. Just as physical things have to be cleaned and maintained, our spirits have to as well.
4. Praying in the Holy Spirit will cleanse our spirits from any and all types of worldly contamination so that seeds of ungodliness will not take root.

Questions and Answers

1. **Who is the Holy Spirit? (Section IA; Page 89)**

    He is the Spirit of God who lives on the inside of the Christian.

2. **What is the function of the Holy Spirit? (Section IIA-C; Page 89)**
    - The Holy Spirit is in partnership with God the Father and God the Son to help carry out the mission of the church.
    - He is the one who empowers, teaches, leads, guides, and comforts (Acts 1:8; Luke 12:12; John 14:26, 16:13).
    - The Holy Spirit is the intercessor praying the perfect will of the Father at all times (Romans 8:26). He is the power source, the anointing (Acts 1:8).

3. **Explain the Baptism of the Holy Spirit in your own words. (Section IIIA; Page 89)**

    The baptism of the Holy Spirit occurs when a Christian receives an overflow of God's Spirit (John 4:13-14, 7:38).

4. **What is the evidence of the Baptism of the Holy Spirit? (Section IIIA; Page 89)**

    The baptism of the Holy Spirit (also referred to as being filled with the Spirit) is evident through speaking in tongues.

5. **What are tongues? (Section IVA; Page 89)**

    Tongues are a heavenly language only God can understand. It cannot be translated, only interpreted as the Holy Spirit reveals.

6. **List the three categories in which tongues can be spoken. (Section VA-C; Page 90)**
   - Private Devotional Time
   - Corporate Worship and Prayer
   - Tongues Draw the Unbeliever

7. **What are the four benefits of speaking in tongues? (Section VI A-D; Page 90)**
   - Spiritual Edification
   - Praying the Perfect Will of God
   - Stimulates Faith
   - Keeps One Free From Spiritual Contamination

VII. HOW TO RECEIVE THE BAPTISM OF THE HOLY SPIRIT

The baptism of the Holy Spirit can be received in a corporate (church or group) setting or individually.

A. It is important that the individual who is receiving the Holy Spirit is a Christian, has repented of all sin, and does not have unforgiveness toward any individuals.

B. This can block the baptism. It is important to understand that the Holy Spirit has already been given (Acts 2:1-4). It is your responsibility to receive the baptism of the Holy Spirit.

C. Be sure that you are not engaging in sinful behavior or harboring unforgiveness. If so, take a moment and repent of sins and release all unforgiveness. If necessary, review the "Repentance" section in chapter 3.

VIII. PRAYER TO RECEIVE THE BAPTISM OF THE HOLY SPIRIT

A. *Lord, please forgive me of my sins (name the sin). I repent and take on the mind of Christ concerning this area of my life. I will commit to aligning my actions with the Word of God so that I will not return to sin. I forgive and release everyone who has offended and/or hurt me in any way. I release all the hurt and every offense knowing You bore it on the cross. By every stripe You endured on the cross I am healed and made whole.*

B. Pray the following prayer (individual): "Lord, I ask that you baptize me in the Holy Spirit."

Pray the following prayer (for someone): "Lord, baptize them in the Holy Spirit."

1. You will hear words in your spirit that will not make sense. That is the heavenly language. Do not analyze or try to figure anything out. It will not make sense to your human intellect.

2. Open your mouth and speak by faith. You will begin to speak in tongues. This is the evidence that you have received the Holy Spirit. Let it flow!
3. After you have received the Holy Spirit pray this prayer: "Lord, give me the gift of tongues so I can speak in the heavenly language at any time."

The same method can be followed if you are assisting someone to receive the baptism of the Holy Spirit.

Chapter 6

The Holy Spirit: The Gifts of the Spirit

This chapter will explain the other benefits of the Holy Spirit. These benefits are referred to as the gifts of the Holy Spirit. These gifts can only be operative to those Christians who have received the baptism or infilling of the Holy Spirit.

These gifts enable the Christian to operate beyond human capacity and in the supernatural. There are many examples of Jesus, the apostles, and Christians operating in the gifts of the Spirit. These examples can be found in any of the Gospels (first four books of the New Testament) and the book of Acts.

The power and anointing the Holy Spirit provides are available to those Christians who move in faith as the Spirit leads and guides.

Any Christian who has been baptized with the Holy Spirit can operate in any of these gifts as the Holy Spirit wills.

The Gifts of the Spirit

The Holy Spirit comes with *gifts* that are purposed to empower the Christian to fulfill the mission of the church, which is winning souls to Christ. The gifts empower the Christian to be victorious in their individual lives and to edify and encourage others. There are nine gifts and they are commonly referred to as "the gifts of the Spirit." *See 1 Corinthians 12:4-11.*

I. REVELATORY GIFTS

The revelatory gifts reveal facts or strategies. These gifts are also called the prophetic gifts. There are many testimonials of how the revelatory gifts can be frequently used to enhance others and the body of Christ.

A. **Word of Knowledge:** Reveals facts (past or present) about a situation or person that would not ordinarily be known. *See John 4:16-19.*

B. **Word of Wisdom:** Provides instructions or a strategy as to how to handle a particular matter. This gift presents the "what, where, when, who, and how."
See Matthew 17:24-27 and Luke 17:11-14.

C. **Discerning of Spirits:** This gift allows a person to physically see spirit beings. These spirits can be heavenly beings (angels) or demonic beings (demons). *See Acts 12:5-11, 16:16-18.*

D. **Prophecy:** This gift foretells future events. *See Isaiah 53 and John 12:27-36.*
Note: Any Christian can operate in this form of simple prophecy. Simple prophecy is for edification, exhortation, and comfort to people (1 Corinthians 14:3). Everyone who operates in simple prophecy is not called to the office of a prophet.

II. MIRACULOUS GIFTS

The miraculous gifts display physical manifestations of the supernatural.

A. **Gift of Faith:** A level of faith that moves into operation when a Christian's individual faith cannot go any further. This is faith that produces miracles. *See John 11:38-44.*

B. **Gift of Healing:** The supernatural manifestation of physical healings. *See Acts 9:36.*

C. **Working of Miracles:** These are occurrences that humans have no control over. They happen supernaturally. *See Luke 9:10-17.*

III. UTTERANCE GIFTS

The utterance gifts are a form of communication spoken outwardly.

A. Different Kinds of Tongues: This gift allows a Christian to speak in a language they do not know. This can be the heavenly language or a foreign language. Refer to chapter 5 for a complete explanation of tongues. *See Acts 2:1-13.*

B. Interpretation of Tongues: When God specifically addresses the church, group, or individual in tongues there will always be an interpretation in the native language so the attendees will be able to understand. *See 1 Corinthians 14:6-18.*

Questions and Answers

1. **What is the purpose of the gifts of the Spirit? (Introduction; Page 98)**
   - The Holy Spirit comes with gifts that are purposed to empower the Christian to fulfill the mission of the church which is winning souls to Christ.
   - The gifts also empower the Christian to be victorious in their individual lives.
   - These gifts enable the Christian to operate beyond human capacity and in the supernatural.

2. **List the three categories of the Gifts of the Spirit. (Sections I-III; Page 98)**
   - Revelatory
   - Miraculous
   - Utterance

3. **List the individual gifts that belong to each category of the Gifts of the Spirit (Page 98).**
   - Revelatory: word of knowledge, word of wisdom, discerning of spirits, prophecy
   - **(Section IA-C)**
   - Miraculous: gift of faith, gift of healing, working of miracles **(Section IIA-C)**
   - Utterance: different kind of tongues and interpretation of tongues **(Section IIIA-B)**

CHAPTER 7

Becoming A New Person In Christ

At the moment of salvation, the spirit of a person becomes renewed in Christ. But they may still have areas that need to be conformed to the Word of God. As a teenager, I made a real commitment to the Lord. I gave God a complete and uncompromising YES! But I still had the desire to listen to music that glorified the works of the flesh. Listening to this type of music fed my flesh and birthed desires to do things that were not godly. My newfound commitment produced a hunger to increase my prayer and study time. After consistently reading and praying, I learned I should not have anything to do with unrighteousness (works that glorify the flesh). The music I was listening to was unrighteous. I immediately removed all ungodly music from my music library. As I grew in prayer and study of the Word, the desire to listen to ungodly music was completely gone.

This is the process of becoming a new person in Christ. God will cleanse the spirit so it will be holy and righteous in Him. 2 Corinthians 5:17 says, *"If any man is in Christ he is a new creature. Old things have passed away; behold, all things have become new."* Becoming **new** means you should now live a life that reflects Christ. This chapter will explain the three parts of the human being and the three parts of the soul. This will provide greater insight into how God created humans.

I. THE HUMAN TRICHOTOMY: SPIRIT, SOUL, AND BODY

A. *Now may the God of peace Himself sanctify you completely; and may your whole spirit, soul, and body be preserved blameless at the coming of our Lord Jesus Christ.*

                                                     1 THESSALONIANS 5:23

B. Human beings have three parts (trichotomy): spirit, soul, and body. This reflects the Trinity (Father, Son, and Holy Spirit) **(103)**.

1. **Spirit:** The real you; your most inner being. This is what gets renewed and rejuvenated by the Spirit of God when you receive salvation (John 3:3).

2. **Soul:** Your soul is made up of three parts: will, intellect, and emotions. This encompasses your decision-making functions, how you think and how you feel (James 1:21; 1 Thessalonians 5:23).

3. **Body:** Your actual physical body. Your body houses your spirit (Genesis 1:26).

C. To truly maximize Christianity, the spirit, soul, and body have to experience salvation. Each part has a function it must fulfill in order to maximize Christianity.

D. If your spirit has not experienced regeneration (salvation) it cannot influence your body and soul. It is impossible. All three parts of your humanity have to be in agreement with the Word of God. The Trinity is the perfect example of agreement.

E. All three functions of the Trinity have to be in agreement to operate in the life of every Christian.
   1. What if God did not send Jesus to earth to save us from our sins? What would it benefit a Christian if Jesus never went to the cross?
   2. In Luke 22:41-42, Jesus clearly had doubts about dying on the cross. *"And He was withdrawn from them about a stone's throw, and He knelt down and prayed, saying, 'Father, if it is Your will, take this cup away from Me; nevertheless not My will, but Yours, be done.'"*
   3. What if the Holy Spirit did not want to come and dwell in the hearts of every Christian, giving them power? We could not maximize our Christianity as God purposed it.

F. Your spirit immediately experiences salvation when you accept and confess Jesus as Lord. The soul and body now have to go through the process of matching what has happened in your spirit.

G. Therefore, it is imperative that you maintain a connection with God in your personal time and by becoming planted in a local church. All three parts that make up your human existence now have to become new in Christ.

H. Having an understanding of how God created humans will help guide you through the process of becoming new. Even if you have been a Christian for a number of years this will provide assistance to receiving salvation in areas of your life where you have not experienced a complete deliverance.

II. THE THREE PARTS OF THE SOUL: WILL, MIND, AND EMOTIONS

A. It is important to delve deeper into the *soul* portion of the human trichotomy **(103)**.
   1. The soul must be submitted to God in order to reflect God. This is the area in which many Christians struggle because there is an unintentional ignorance that this area does not need to experience salvation or that it automatically gets in order at conversion.
   2. Many people carry traumatic experiences, childhood occurrences, and past hurts in their souls.
   3. Full submission to God in the area of the soul will result in a healthy relationship with God, oneself, and others. This is why it is important to become planted in a local church. This will provide an opportunity to receive individual counseling to obtain deliverance in specific areas.

B. Will: This function has to do with your decision-making faculties **(103)**.
   1. If your will is not aligned or in agreement with God's will, you will not fulfill the perfect will of God for your life.
   2. Are your desires aligned with the Word of God and God's perfect will for your life? If not, you have some submitting (willful yielding) to do.
   See Psalm 40:8, 143:10; Matthew 12:47-50; Luke 22:42; and John 4:34, 5:30, 6:38.

C. Mind: This function of the soul has to do with your thought and decision-making faculties **(103-104)**.
   1. Are your thinking and decision making founded upon biblical principles? Are your thinking and decision making inspired by the Holy Spirit?
   2. It all revolves around having the mind of Christ.
   3. Jesus instructs us in Philippians 2:5 to have the same mind as His (paraphrased).
   4. If you are thinking like Jesus you will be like Jesus.
   5. Therefore, everything in the Word will manifest itself in your life. Wow! What an overflow and great life to live! *See Psalm 55:18; Proverbs 23:7; Romans 12:2; 1 Corinthians 13:5; Ephesians 4:12; and Philippians 2:5.*

D. Emotions: This function of the soul has to do with your feelings **(104)**.
   1. It is important to walk in spiritual maturity and godly wisdom when dealing with your emotions.
   2. It is necessary to have your emotions girded and submitted to the Word of God so that your thoughts and behavior remain disciplined and under the control of the Holy Spirit (Ephesians 4:17-19).

III. THE PHYSICAL BODY

A. In chapter 1, we read that salvation is for the whole person: spirit, soul, and body. Just as the soul must be submitted to God your physical body must also be submitted to God to reflect salvation and godly behavior.

B. Can the physical body experience salvation and regeneration as the spirit man does?
   1. Yes, when it is submitted to the Word of God. Your body will complete actions based upon commands from the brain.

C. When you receive salvation your spirit, soul, and body should be submitted to the Word of God. Submission to the Word of God will produce godly decisions with corresponding physical actions.

D. *I appeal to you therefore, brethren, and beg of you in view of [all] the mercies of God, to make a decisive dedication of your bodies [presenting all your members and faculties] as a living sacrifice, holy (devoted, consecrated) and well pleasing to God, which is your reasonable (rational, intelligent) service and spiritual worship.*

Do not be conformed to this world (this age), [fashioned after and adapted to its external, superficial customs], but be transformed (changed) by the [entire] renewal of your mind [by its new ideals and its new attitude], so that you may prove [for yourselves] what is the good and acceptable and perfect will of God, even the thing which is good and acceptable and perfect [in His sight for you].   ROMANS 12:1-2 AMP

Questions and Answers

1. **List the three parts of the _human trichotomy_. (Section IA; Page 105)**
   - Spirit
   - Soul
   - Body

2. **Why is it important for all three parts of the _human trichotomy_ to experience salvation? (Section IC; Page 105)**
   If your spirit has not experienced regeneration (salvation) it cannot influence your body and soul. It is impossible. All three parts of your humanity have to be in agreement with the Word of God. The Trinity is the perfect example of agreement.

3. **Why is it important for all three parts of the _soul_ to experience salvation? (Section IIA:1; Page 105)**
   - The soul must be submitted to God in order to reflect God. This is the area in which many Christians struggle because there is an unintentional ignorance that this area does not need to experience salvation or that it automatically gets in order at conversion.
   - It is important for the soul to experience salvation so that the Christian will make Godly decisions (will), think Godly (mind), and have feelings submitted to the Word of God (emotions).

   This answer is not in the outline. However, it summarizes an accurate answer someone may have. Be sure to place emphasis on this point during teaching and group discussion.

4. **List the three parts of the human _soul_ and briefly explain their function (Page 105).**
   - **Will:** This function has to do with your decision-making faculties. **(Section IIB)**
   - **Mind:** This function of the soul has to do with your thought and decision-making faculties. **(Section IIC)**

- **Emotions:** This function of the soul has to do with your feelings. **(Section IID)**

5. **Can the physical body experience salvation as the spirit man does (Page 106)? (Section IIIB)**

   Yes, when it is submitted to the Word of God. Your body will complete actions based upon commands from the brain.

Self-Check

6. Assess each part of your soul (will, mind, emotions). List the areas that are not functioning according to the Word of God. The questions listed below will help begin the assessment. Do not allow the starter questions to limit your assessment (Page 106).

Will
- Do I reverence (honor, respect) God?
- Do I obey the Word of God?

Mind
- Are my thoughts godly?
- Is my perspective of life, people, and situations viewed from the perspective of the Word of God?

Emotions
- Do I harbor unforgiveness?
- Do I treat people with godly love?
- Do I respond with emotional maturity to challenging situations?
- Am I always angry?
- Am I fearful?

Refer to the **Group Leader Suggestions** *listed in the* **How to Use Transformation Leader Edition** *section located at the beginning of the curriculum.*

NOTES

Chapter 1

1. Sonya Ellerbe, *"Work It Out"* (sermon presentation, United Christian Fellowship Church International, Salisbury, NC, March 15, 2015).

2. *KJV New Testament Greek Lexicon*, s.v. "Anothen," accessed February 13, 2015, http://www.biblestudytools.com/lexicons/greek/nas/anothen.html.

Chapter 3

3. *KJV New Testament Greek Lexicon*, s.v. "Katergazomai," accessed February 13, 2015, http://www.biblestudytools.com/lexicons/greek/kjv/katergazomai.html.

4. *KJV New Testament Greek Lexicon*, s.v. "Christianos," accessed February 13, 2015, http://www.biblestudytools.com/lexicons/greek/kjv/christianos.html.

5. Dennis Clark, interviewed by Sid Roth. Online, *God's Presence 24/7*, http://www.youtube.com, November 5, 2012.

Chapter 4

6. Charlton T. Lewis and Charles Short. *A Latin Dictionary*. Accessed March 19, 2015. http://www.latin-dictionary.net.

ABOUT THE AUTHOR

Trina Nichelle Moore currently serves as the Director of Ministries and Minister of Christian Education at United Christian Fellowship Church International (UCFCI), Salisbury, North Carolina, under the leadership of Pastor Sonya T. Ellerbe. Her education accolades include a Bachelor of Arts degree in Music Education from Livingstone College, Salisbury, North Carolina, and a Master degree in School Administration from the University of North Carolina at Charlotte.

While serving as Minister of Christian Education, her other responsibilities include music ministry, community outreach efforts, and the development of new ministry opportunities discovered both in the church and community. Trina has eleven years of teaching experience as a choral music teacher in Rowan-Salisbury Schools and Charlotte-Mecklenburg Schools. As choral director at Martin Luther King Jr. Middle School (MLK) in Charlotte, North Carolina, she composed the song titled "Purpose." This inspirational song became MLK's official school song in the spring of 2011. Along with local radio support and internet radio airplay, the single was heard in the United States and thirty-seven international countries. Further support was garnered on local TV-WCNC Channel 36 with a feature on the evening news and a performance on the morning talk show "Charlotte Today." The school song continues to be played every school day.

As Minister of Christian Education, Trina trains those called to the equipping office of the teaching ministry. She also develops curriculum to address the specific spiritual needs of UCFCI. Trina's first published work is titled *Be Like Jesus Scriptures for Transformation*. It is a collection of Scriptures outlined to the lyrics of the song "Be Like Jesus," released in 2013. This upbeat, contemporary single is rich with soulful ad-libs and eloquent phrases that highlight the incredible experience of newness and wholeness that are only available through salvation in Jesus Christ. This eight-chapter book also includes Scriptures on topics such as salvation, healing, financial integrity, and much more.

Trina's second published work, *Transformation,* is a study guide explaining in detail the foundational principles of Christianity such as salvation, maintaining salvation, and repentance. It is a must read for new Christians, recommitted Christians, and seasoned Christians. United Christian Fellowship Church International (www.ucfci.org) has adopted *Transformation* as the official curriculum for its Christian Living classes (for new and recommitted Christians). Both books are published by Degel Publishing, which Trina owns independently.

The biblical principle found in Matthew 22:37 (NKJV) serves as the motivating foundation for Trina in life and ministry: *"You shall love the Lord your God with all your heart, with all your soul, and with all your mind."* This biblical command birthed Trina's purpose for ministry. That purpose is to give God all the glory, unite and reunite souls with Christ, and encourage the body of Christ. Trina currently resides in Charlotte, North Carolina. For more information visit www.trinanichellemoore.com.

www.ingramcontent.com/pod-product-compliance
Lightning Source LLC
Chambersburg PA
CBHW080409300426
44113CB00015B/2456